THE PILGRIMAGE

PAULO COELHO

THE PILGRIMAGE

TRANSLATED BY ALAN R. CLARKE

HarperCollins*Publishers*

HarperCollins*Publishers*
77–85 Fulham Palace Road,
Hammersmith, London W6 8JB

HarperCollins website address is:
www.harpercollins.co.uk
Paulo Coelho's website address is:
http://www.paulocoelho.com.br

Originally published in Portuguese as *O diario de um Mago*
by Editora Rocco Ltd, Rio de Janeiro 1987
English version first published as *The Diary of a Magus* 1992
Published in paperback by HarperCollins Publishers, USA 1995
Published by HarperCollins Publishers, UK 1997
This edition published 2003

20

English version © Paulo Coelho and Alan R. Clarke 1992

Paulo Coelho asserts the moral right to
be identified as the author of this work

A catalogue record for this book
is available from the British Library

ISBN 0 7225 3487 6

Printed and bound in Great Britain by
Clays Ltd, St Ives plc

Contents

The Pilgrimage

Prologue

And now, before the sacred countenance of RAM, you must touch with your hands the Word of Life and acquire such power as you need to become a witness to that Word throughout the world."

The Master raised high my new sword, still sheathed in its scabbard. The flames of the bonfire crackled—a good omen, indicating that the ritual should continue. I knelt and, with my bare hands, began to dig into the earth.

It was the night of January 2, 1986, and we were in Itatiaia, high on one of the peaks in the Serra do Mar, close to the formation known as the Agulhas Negras (Black Needles) in Brazil. My Master and I were accompanied by my wife, one of my disciples, a local guide, and a representative of the great fraternity that is comprised of esoteric orders from all over the world—the fraternity known as "the Tradition." The five of us—and the guide, who had been told what was to happen—were participating in my ordination as a Master of the Order of RAM.

I finished digging a smooth, elongated hole in the dirt. With great solemnity, I placed my hands on the earth and spoke the ritual words. My wife drew near and handed me the sword I had used for more than ten years; it had been a great help to me during hundreds of magical operations. I placed it in the hole I had dug, covered it with dirt, and smoothed the surface. As I did so, I thought of the many tests I had endured, of all I had learned, and of the strange phenomena I had been able to invoke simply because I had had that ancient and friendly sword with me. Now it was to be devoured by the earth, the iron of its blade and the wood of its hilt returning to nourish the source from which its power had come.

The Master approached me and placed my new sword on the earth that now covered the grave of my ancient one. All of us spread our arms wide, and the Master, invoking his power, created a strange light that surrounded us; it did not illuminate, but it was clearly visible, and it caused the figures of those who were there to take on a color that was different from the yellowish tinge cast by the fire. Then, drawing his own sword, he touched it to my shoulders and my forehead as he said, "By the power and the love of RAM, I anoint you Master and Knight of the Order, now and for all the days of your life. R for rigor, A for adoration, and M for mercy; R for *regnum*, A for *agnus*, and M for *mundi*. Let not your sword remain for long in its scabbard, lest it rust. And when you draw your sword, it must never be replaced without having performed an act of goodness, opened a new path, or tasted the blood of an enemy."

With the point of his sword, he lightly cut my forehead. From then on, I was no longer required to remain silent. No longer did I have to hide my capabilities nor maintain secrecy regarding the marvels I had learned to accomplish on the road of the Tradition. From that moment on, I was a Magus.

I reached out to take my new sword of indestructible steel and wood, with its black and red hilt and black scabbard.

But as my hands touched the scabbard and as I prepared to pick it up, the Master came forward and stepped on my fingers with all his might. I screamed and let go of the sword.

I looked at him, astonished. The strange light had disappeared, and his face had taken on a phantasmagoric appearance, heightened by the flames of the bonfire.

He returned my gaze coldly, called to my wife, and gave her the sword, speaking a few words that I could not hear. Turning to me, he said, "Take away your hand; it has deceived you. The road of the Tradition is not for the chosen few. It is everyone's road. And the power that you think you have is worthless, because it is a power that is shared by all. You should have refused the sword. If you had done so, it would have been given to you, because you would have shown that your heart was pure. But just as I feared, at the supreme moment you stumbled and fell. Because of your avidity, you will now have to seek again for your sword. And because of your pride, you will have to seek it among simple people. Because of your fascination with miracles, you will have to struggle to recapture what was about to be given to you so generously."

The world seemed to fall away from me. I knelt there unable to think about anything. Once I had returned my old sword to the earth, I could not retrieve it. And since the new one had not been given to me, I now had to begin my quest for it all over again, powerless and defenseless. On the day of my Celestial Ordination, my Master's violence had brought me back to earth.

The guide smothered the fire, and my wife helped me up. She had my new sword in her hands, but according to the rules of the Tradition, I could not touch it without permission from my Master. We descended through the forest in silence, following the guide's lantern, until we reached the narrow dirt road where the cars were parked.

Nobody said good-bye. My wife put the sword in the trunk of the car and started the engine. We were quiet for a long time as she carefully navigated around the bumps and holes in the road.

"Don't worry," she said, trying to encourage me. "I'm sure you'll get it back."

I asked her what the Master had said to her.

"He said three things to me. First, that he should have brought along something warm to wear, because it was much colder up there than he had expected. Second, that he wasn't surprised at anything that had happened up there, that this has happened many times before with others who have reached the same point as you. And third, that your sword would be waiting for you at the right time, on the right day, at some point on the road that you will have to travel. I don't know either the day or the time. He only told me where I should hide it."

"And what road was he talking about?" I asked nervously.

"Ah, well, that he didn't explain very well. He just said that you should look on the map of Spain for a medieval route known as the Strange Road to Santiago."

THE ROAD TO SANTIAGO

Arrival

🌀

The customs agent spent more time than usual examining the sword that my wife had brought into the country and then asked what we intended to do with it. I said that a friend of ours was going to assess its value so that we could sell it at auction. This lie worked: the agent gave us a declaration stating that we had entered the country with the sword at the Bajadas airport, and he told us that if we had any problems trying to leave the country with it, we need only show the declaration to the customs officials.

. We went to the car rental agency and confirmed our two vehicles. Armed with the rental documents, we had a bite together at the airport restaurant prior to going our separate ways.

We had spent a sleepless night on the plane—the result of both a fear of flying and a sense of apprehension about what was going to happen once we arrived—but now we were excited and wide awake.

"Not to worry," she said for the thousandth time. "You're supposed to go to France and, at Saint-Jean-Pied-de-Port, seek out Mme Lourdes. She is going to put you in touch with someone who will guide you along the Road to Santiago."

"And what about you?" I asked, also for the thousandth time, knowing what her answer would be.

"I'm going where I have to go, and there I'll leave what has been entrusted to me. Afterward, I'll spend a few days in Madrid and then return to Brazil. I can take care of things back there as well as you would."

"I know you can," I answered, wanting to avoid the subject. I felt an enormous anxiety about the business matters I had left behind in Brazil. I had learned all I needed to know about the Road to Santiago in the fifteen days following the incident in the Agulhas Negras, but I had vacillated for another seven months before deciding to leave everything behind and make the trip. I had put it off until one morning when my wife had said that the time was drawing near and that if I did not make a decision, I might as well forget about the road of the Tradition and the Order of RAM. I had tried to explain to her that my Master had assigned me an impossible task, that I couldn't simply shrug off my livelihood. She had smiled and said that my excuse was dumb, that during the entire seven months I had done nothing but ask myself night and day whether or not I should go. And with the most casual of gestures, she had held out the two airline tickets, with the flight already scheduled.

"We're here because of your decision," I said glumly now in the airport restaurant. "I don't know if this will even work, since I let another person make the decision for me to seek out my sword."

My wife said that if we were going to start talking nonsense, we had better say good-bye and go our separate ways.

"You have never in your life let another person make an important decision for you. Let's go. It's getting late." She rose, picked up her suitcase, and headed for the parking lot.

I didn't stop her. I stayed seated, observing the casual way in which she carried my sword; at any moment it seemed that it could slip from under her arm.

She stopped suddenly, came back to the table, and kissed me desperately. She looked at me for some time without saying a word. This suddenly made me realize that now I was actually in Spain and that there was no going back. In spite of the knowledge that there were many ways in which I could fail, I had taken the first step. I hugged her passionately, trying to convey all the love I felt for her at that moment. And while she was still in my arms, I prayed to everything and everyone I believed in, imploring that I be given the strength to return to her with the sword.

"That was a beautiful sword, wasn't it?" said a woman's voice from the next table, after my wife had left.

"Don't worry," a man said. "I'll buy one just like it for you. The tourist shops here in Spain have thousands of them."

After I had driven for an hour or so, I began to feel the fatigue accumulated from the night before. The August heat was so powerful that even on the open highway, the car began to overheat. I decided to stop in a small town identified by the road signs as Monumento Nacional. As I climbed the steep road that led to it, I began to review all that I had learned about the Road to Santiago.

Just as the Muslim tradition requires that all members of the faith, at least once in their life, make the same pilgrimage that Muhammad made from Mecca to Medina, so Christians in the first millennium considered three routes to be sacred. Each of them offered a series of blessings and indulgences to those who traveled its length. The first led to the tomb of Saint Peter in Rome; its travelers, who were called wanderers, took the cross as their symbol. The second led to the Holy Sepulcher of Christ in Jerusalem; those who took this road were called palmists, since they had as their symbol the palm branches with which Jesus was greeted when he entered that city. There was a third road, which led to the mortal remains of the apostle, San Tiago—Saint James in English, Jacques in French, Giacomo in Italian, Jacob in Latin. He was buried at a place on the Iberian peninsula where, one night, a shepherd had seen a brilliant star above a field. The legend says that not only San Tiago but also the Virgin Mary went there shortly after the death of Christ, carrying the word of the Evangelist and exhorting the people to convert. The site came to be known as Compostela—the star field— and there a city had arisen that drew travelers from every part of the Christian world. These travelers were called pilgrims, and their symbol was the scallop shell.

At the height of its fame, during the fourteenth century, the Milky Way—another name for the third road, since at night the pilgrims plotted their course using this galaxy—was traveled each year by more than a million people from every corner of Europe. Even today, mystics, devotees, and researchers traverse on foot the seven hundred kilometers that separate the French city of Saint-Jean-Pied-de-Port from the cathedral of Santiago de Compostela in Spain.[1]

Thanks to the French priest, Aymeric Picaud, who walked to Compostela in 1123, the route followed by the pilgrims today is exactly the same as the medieval path taken by Charlemagne, Saint Francis of Assisi, Isabella of Castile, and, most recently, by Pope John XXIII.

Picaud wrote five books about his experience. They were presented as the work of Pope Calixtus II—a devotee of San

---

[1]The Road to Santiago, on the French side, was comprised of several routes that joined at a Spanish city called Puente de la Reina. The city of Saint-Jean-Pied-de-Port is located on one of those three routes; it is neither the only one nor the most important.

Tiago—and they were later known as the Codex Calixtinus. In Book Five of the codex, Picaud identified the natural features, fountains, hospitals, shelters, and cities found along the road. A special society—"Les Amis de Saint-Jacques"—was then formed with the charge of maintaining all of the natural markings on the route and helping to guide the pilgrims, using Picaud's annotations.

Also in the twelfth century, Spain began to capitalize on the legend of San Tiago as the country fought against the Moors who had invaded the peninsula. Several militant religious orders were established along the Road to Santiago, and the apostle's ashes became a powerful symbol in the fight against the Muslims. The Muslims, in turn, claimed that they had with them one of Muhammad's arms and took that as their guiding symbol. By the time Spain had regained control of the country, the militant orders had become so strong that they posed a threat to the nobility, and the Catholic kings had to intervene directly to prevent the orders from mounting an insurgency. As a result, the Road to Santiago was gradually forgotten, and were it not for sporadic artistic manifestations—in paintings such as Buñuel's *The Milky Way* and Juan Manoel Serrat's *Wanderer*—no one today would remember that millions of the people who would one day settle the New World had passed along that route.

The town that I reached by car was completely deserted. After searching on foot for quite some time, I finally found a small bar open for business in an old, medieval-style house. The owner, who did not even look up from the television program he was watching, advised me that it was siesta time and suggested that I must be crazy to be out walking in such heat.

I asked for a soft drink and tried to watch television, but I was unable to concentrate. All I could think of was that in two days, I was going to relive, here in the latter part of the twentieth century, something of the great human adventure that had brought Ulysses from Troy, that had been a part of Don Quixote's experience, that had led Dante and Orpheus into hell, and that had directed Columbus to the Americas: the adventure of traveling toward the unknown.

By the time I returned to my car, I was a bit calmer. Even if I were not able to find my sword, the pilgrimage along the Road to Santiago was going to help me to find myself.

Saint-Jean-Pied-de-Port

(6)

A parade of masked people accompanied by a band—all of them dressed in red, green, and white, the colors of the French Basque region—filled the main street of Saint-Jean-Pied-de-Port. It was Sunday. I had spent the last two days driving, and now I was enjoying the festivities. But it was time for my meeting with Mme Lourdes. Forcing my way through the crowd by car, I heard some shouted insults in French, but I finally made it through to the fortified sector that constituted the oldest part of the city, where Mme Lourdes lived. Even this high in the Pyrenees, it was hot during the day, and I was soaked with perspiration as I got out of the car.

I knocked at the gate. I knocked again, but there was no response. A third time, and still nothing happened. I felt confused and worried. My wife had said that I had to arrive there exactly on that day, but no one answered when I called out. I thought that perhaps Mme Lourdes had gone out to watch the parade, but it was also possible that I had arrived too late and that she had decided not to meet with me. My journey along the Road to Santiago seemed to have ended even before it had begun.

Suddenly, the gate opened, and a child jumped through it. I was startled, and in halting French I asked for Mme Lourdes. The child smiled at me and pointed toward the house. It was only then that I saw my mistake: the gate led onto an immense courtyard, around which were situated medieval houses with balconies. The gate had been open, and I hadn't even thought to try its handle.

I ran across the courtyard and up to the house that the child had indicated. Inside, an elderly, obese woman yelled something in Basque at a small boy with sad, brown eyes. I waited for a few moments, giving the argument a chance to end; it finally did, with the poor boy being sent to the kitchen under a hail of insults from the old woman. It was only then that she turned to me and, without even asking what it was that I wanted, led me—with delicate gestures and slight shoves—to the second floor of the small house. This floor consisted of just one room: a small, crowded office filled with books, objects, statues of San Tiago, and memorabilia from the Road. She took a book from its shelf and sat down behind the only table in the room, leaving me standing.

"You must be another pilgrim to Santiago," she said, without preamble. "I need to enter your name in the register of those who walk the Road."

I gave her my name, and she wanted to know if I had brought "the Scallops." She was referring to the shells adopted as a symbol by pilgrims to the tomb of the apostle; they served as a means of identification for the pilgrims when they met.[1]

---

[1]The Road to Santiago has made only one mark on French culture, and that has been on that country's national pride, gastronomy, through the name "Coquilles Saint-Jacques."

Before leaving for Spain, I had made a pilgrimage to a place in Brazil called Aparecida do Norte. There, I had purchased an image of Our Lady of the Visitation, mounted on three scallop shells. I took it from my knapsack and offered it to Mme Lourdes.

"Pretty but not very practical," she said, handing it back to me. "It could break during your pilgrimage."

"It's not going to break. And I am going to leave it at the tomb of the apostle."

Mme Lourdes appeared not to have much time for me. She gave me a small card that would help me to get lodging at the monasteries along the Road, stamped it with the seal of Saint-Jean-Pied-de-Port to indicate that I had started the pilgrimage there, and said that I could leave with God's blessing.

"But where is my guide?" I asked.

"What guide?" she answered, a bit surprised but also with a gleam in her eye.

I realized that I had forgotten something very important. In my eagerness to arrive and be attended to, I had neglected to say the Ancient Word—a kind of password that identifies those who belong to the orders of the Tradition. I immediately corrected my mistake and said the word to her. In response, Mme Lourdes quickly snatched from my hands the card she had given me a few moments earlier.

"You won't be needing this," she said, as she moved a pile of old newspapers that were sitting on top of a cardboard box. "Your road and your stopping places will depend on decisions made by your guide."

Mme Lourdes took a hat and a cape from the box. They seemed to be very old but well preserved. She asked me to stand in the middle of the room, and she began silently to pray. Then she placed the cape on my shoulders and the hat on my head. I could see that scallop shells had been sewn onto both the hat and the shoulders of the cape. Without interrupting her prayers, the old woman seized a shepherd's crook from the corner of the room and made me take it in my right hand. A small water gourd hung from the crook. There I stood: dressed in Bermuda shorts and a T-shirt that read "I LOVE NY," covered by the medieval garb of the pilgrims to Compostela.

The old woman approached me and stopped only a foot away. Then, in a kind of trance, placing the palms of her hands on my head, she said, "May the apostle San Tiago be with you, and may he show you the only thing that you need to discover; may you walk neither too slowly nor too fast but always according to the laws and the requirements of the Road; may you obey the one who is your guide, even though he may issue an order that is homicidal, blasphemous, or senseless. You must swear total obedience to your guide."

I so swore.

"The Spirit of the ancient pilgrims of the Tradition must be with you during your journey. The hat will protect you from the sun and from evil thoughts; the cape will protect you from the rain and from evil words; the gourd will protect you from enemies and from evil deeds. May the blessing of God, of San Tiago, and of the Virgin Mary be with you through all of your nights and days. Amen."

Having said this, she returned to her normal manner: hurriedly and with a bit of irritation, she took back the articles of clothing, placed them in the box, and returned the crook with the gourd to the corner of the room; then, after teaching me the password, she asked me to leave, since my guide was waiting for me two kilometers outside of Saint-Jean-Pied-de-Port.

"He hates band music," she said. But even two kilometers away he must have been able to hear it; the Pyrenees are an excellent echo chamber.

Before I left, I asked what I should do with the car, and she said I should leave the keys with her; someone would come to pick it up. Then, without another word, she descended the stairs and went to the kitchen to inflict more torment on the boy with the sad eyes. I opened the trunk of the car, took out my small blue knapsack with my sleeping bag tied to it, and placed the image of Our Lady of the Visitation in its most protected corner. I put the knapsack on my back and went back to give the keys to Mme Lourdes.

"Leave Pied-de-Port by following this street to the city gates at the end of the wall," she told me. "And when you get to Santiago de Compostela, say a Hail Mary for me. I have walked the Road so many times that now I content myself with reading in other pilgrims' eyes the excitement that I still feel; I just can't put it into practice anymore because of my age. Tell that to San Tiago. And tell him also that any time now I will join him, following a different road that's more direct and less exhausting."

I left the small city, passing through the wall at the Spanish Gate. In the past, the city had been on the preferred route for the Roman invaders, and through that gate had also passed the armies of Charlemagne and Napoleon. I walked along, hearing the band music in the distance, and suddenly, in the ruins of a village not far from the city, I was overwhelmed by emotion, and my eyes filled with tears: there in the ruins, the full impact of the fact that I was walking the Strange Road to Santiago finally hit me.

The view of the Pyrenees surrounding the valley, lit by the morning sun and intensified by the sound of the music, gave me the sensation that I was returning to something primitive, something that had been forgotten by most other human beings, something that I was unable to identify. But it was a strange and powerful feeling, and I decided to quicken my pace and arrive as soon as possible at the place where Mme Lourdes had said my guide would be waiting for me. Without stopping, I took off my shirt and put it in my knapsack. The straps cut into my bare shoulders a bit, but at least my old sneakers were broken in enough that they caused me no discomfort. After almost forty minutes, at a curve in the road that circled around a gigantic rock, I came upon an old abandoned well. There, sitting on the ground, was a man of about fifty; he had black hair and the look of a gypsy, and he was searching for something in his knapsack.

"*Hola*," I said in Spanish, with the same timidity that I show whenever I meet anyone new. "You must be waiting for me. My name is Paulo."

The man interrupted his search through the knapsack and looked me up and down. His gaze was cold, and he seemed not at all surprised by my arrival. I also had the vague impression that I knew him.

"Yes, I was waiting for you, but I didn't know that I was going to meet you so soon. What do you want?"

I was a little disconcerted by his question and answered that it was I whom he was to guide along the Milky Way in search of my sword.

"That's not necessary," said the man. "If you want me to, I can find it for you. But you have to decide right now whether you want me to."

This conversation with the stranger seemed increasingly weird to me. But since I had sworn complete obedience, I tried to respond. If he could find my sword for me, it would save an enormous amount of time, and I could return immediately to my friends and my business in Brazil; they were always on my mind. This could also be a trick, but there was no harm in giving him an answer.

As I was about to say yes, I heard a voice behind me say, in heavily accented Spanish, "You don't have to climb a mountain to find out whether or not it's high."

It was the password! I turned and saw a man of about forty, in khaki Bermudas and a white, sweaty T-shirt, staring at the gypsy. He was gray-haired, and his skin was darkened by the sun. In my haste, I had forgotten the most elementary rules of self-protection and had thrown myself body and soul into the arms of the first stranger I had met.

"The ship is safest when it's in port, but that's not what ships were built for," I said, as the correct response. Meanwhile, the man looked directly at the gypsy and the gypsy stared at the man. Both confronted each other, with no sign of fear or challenge, for some time. Then the gypsy left the knapsack on the ground, smiled disdainfully, and walked off in the direction of Saint-Jean-Pied-de-Port.

"My name is Petrus,"[2] said the new arrival as soon as the gypsy had disappeared behind the huge stone that I had circled a few minutes earlier. "Next time, be more cautious."

I heard a sympathetic tone in his voice; it was different from the tone of the gypsy and of Mme Lourdes. He lifted the knapsack from the ground, and I noticed that it had the scallop shell on its back. He produced a bottle of wine, took a swallow, and offered it to me. After I had taken a drink, I asked him who the gypsy was.

"This is a frontier route often used by smugglers and terrorist refugees from the Spanish Basque country," said Petrus. "The police hardly ever come near here."

[2]Actually, Petrus told me his real name. I have changed it in order to protect his privacy, but this is one of the few times that names have been changed in this book.

"But you're not answering me. You two looked at each other like old acquaintances. And I had the feeling that I knew him, too. That's why I was so much at ease."

Petrus smiled and said that we should move along. I picked up my things, and we began to walk in silence. From Petrus's smile I knew that he was thinking the same thing I was.

We had met with a devil.

We walked along without talking for a while, and I could see that Mme Lourdes had been right: from almost three kilometers away, we could still hear the sound of the band. I wanted to ask some questions of Petrus—about his life, his work, and what had brought him here. I knew, though, that we still had seven hundred kilometers to cover together and that the appropriate moment would come for having all of my questions answered. But I could not get the gypsy out of my mind, and finally I broke the silence.

"Petrus, I think that the gypsy was the devil."

"Yes, he was the devil." When he confirmed this, I felt a mixture of terror and relief. "But he isn't the devil that you know from the Tradition."

In the Tradition, the devil is a spirit that is neither good nor evil; he is considered to be the guardian of most of the secrets that are accessible to human beings and to have strength and power over material things. Since he is a fallen angel, he is identified with the human race, and he is always ready to make deals and exchange favors. I asked what was the difference between the gypsy and the devil of the Tradition.

"We are going to meet others along the Road," he smiled. "You will see for yourself. But just to give you an idea, try to remember your entire conversation with the gypsy."

I reviewed the two phrases I had heard from him. He had said that he was waiting for me and had affirmed that he would seek out the sword for me.

Then Petrus said that those two phrases fit perfectly well in the mouth of a thief who had been surprised in the act of robbing a knapsack: they were aimed at gaining time and at winning favor while he quickly figured out a means of escape. On the other hand, the two phrases could mean exactly what they said.

"Which is right?"

"Both are true. That poor thief, while he defended himself, picked out of the air the very words that needed to be said to you. He thought that he was being intelligent, but he was really acting as the instrument of a greater power. If he had fled when I arrived, we wouldn't be having this conversation now. But he confronted me, and I read in his eyes the name of a devil that you are going to meet somewhere along the Road."

For Petrus, the meeting had been a favorable omen, since the devil had revealed himself so early.

"Meanwhile, don't worry about him because, as I have already told you, he won't be the only one. He may be the most important one, but he won't be the only one."

We continued walking, passing from a desertlike area to one where small trees were scattered here and there. Once in a while Petrus broke the silence to tell me some historic fact or other about the places we were passing. I saw the house where a queen had spent the last night of her life and a small chapel encrusted with rocks, which had been the hermitage of a saintly man who the few inhabitants of the area swore could perform miracles.

"Miracles are very important, don't you think?" Petrus said.

I agreed but said that I had never witnessed a great miracle. My apprenticeship in the Tradition had been much more on the intellectual plane. I believed that when I recovered my sword, then, yes, I would be capable of doing the great deeds that my Master did.

"But what my Master performs are not miracles, because they don't contradict the laws of nature. What my Master does is utilize these forces to . . ."

I couldn't finish the sentence because I couldn't explain how my Master had been able to materialize spirits, move objects from one place to another without touching them, or, as I had witnessed more than once, create patches of blue sky on a cloudy afternoon.

"Maybe he does those things simply to convince you that he has the knowledge and the power," answered Petrus.

"Yes, maybe so," I said, without much conviction.

We sat down on a stone because Petrus told me that he hated to smoke cigarettes while he was walking. According to him, the lungs absorbed much more nicotine if one smoked while walking, and the smoke nauseated him.

"That was why the Master refused to let you have the sword," Petrus continued. "Because you didn't understand why he performs his prodigious feats. Because you forgot that the path to knowledge is a path that's open to everyone, to the common people. During our journey, I'm going to teach you some exercises and some rituals that are known as the practices of RAM. All of us, at some time in our lives, have made use of at least one of them. Every one of these practices, without exception, can be discovered by anyone who is willing to seek them out, with patience and perspicacity, among the lessons that life itself teaches us.

"The RAM practices are so simple that people like you, who are used to making life too complicated, ascribe little value to them. But it is they that make people capable of achieving anything, absolutely anything, that they desire.

"Jesus glorified the Father when his disciples began to perform miracles and cures; he thanked God for having kept such things secret from wise people and for revealing them to simple folk. When all is said and done, if we believe in God, we have to believe also that God is just."

Petrus was absolutely right. It would be a divine injustice to allow only those people who were learned and who had the time and money to buy expensive books to have access to true knowledge.

"The true path to wisdom can be identified by three things," said Petrus. "First, it must involve agape, and I'll tell you more about this later; second, it has to have practical application in your life. Otherwise, wisdom becomes a useless thing and deteriorates, like a sword that is never used.

"And finally, it has to be a path that can be followed by anyone. Like the road you are walking now, the Road to Santiago."

We walked for the rest of the afternoon, and only when the sun began to disappear behind the mountains did Petrus decide to stop again. All around us the highest peaks of the Pyrenees still shone in the last light of day.

Petrus told me to clear a small area on the ground and to kneel there.

"The first RAM practice will help you to achieve rebirth. You will have to do the exercise for seven consecutive days, each time trying to experience in some different way your first contact with the world. You know how difficult it was for you to make the decision to drop everything and come here to walk the Road to Santiago in search of a sword. But this was difficult only because you were a prisoner of the past. You had been defeated before, and you were afraid that it could happen again. You had already achieved things, and you were afraid you might lose them. But at the same time, something stronger than any of that prevailed: the desire to find your sword. So you decided to take the risk."

I said that he was right but that I still had the worries he described.

"That doesn't matter. The exercise, little by little, will free you from the burdens that you have created in your life."

And Petrus taught me the first RAM practice: the Seed Exercise.

"Do it now for the first time," he said.

I lowered my head between my knees, breathed deeply, and began to relax. My body obeyed without question, perhaps because we had walked so far during the day and I was exhausted. I began to listen to the sound of the earth, muffled and harsh, and bit by bit I transformed myself into a seed. I didn't think. Everything was dark, and I was asleep at the center of the earth. Suddenly, something moved. It was a part of me, a minuscule part of me that wanted to awaken, that said that I had to leave this place because there was something else "up there." I wanted to sleep, but this part insisted. I began to move my fingers, and my fingers began to move my arms—but they were neither fingers nor arms. They were a small shoot that was fighting to overcome the force of the earth and to move in the direction of that "something up there." I felt my body begin to follow the movement of my arms. Each second seemed like an eternity, but the seed needed to be born; it needed to know what that "something up there" was. With immense difficulty, my head, then my body, began to rise. Everything was too slow, and I had to fight against the force that was pushing me down toward the center of the earth where before I had been tranquil, dreaming an eternal dream. But I was winning, I was winning, and finally I broke through something and was upright. The force that had been pressing down on me suddenly ceased. I had broken through the earth and was surrounded by that "something up there."

The "something up there" was the field. I sensed the heat of the sun, the hum of the mosquitoes, the sound of a

THE SEED EXERCISE

Kneel on the ground. Then seat yourself on your heels and bend forward so that your head touches your knees. Stretch your arms behind you. You are now in a fetal position. Relax, releasing all of your tensions. Breathe calmly and deeply. Little by little you will perceive that you are a tiny seed, cradled in the comfort of the earth. Everything around you is warm and delicious. You are in a deep, restful sleep.

Suddenly, a finger moves. The shoot no longer wants to be a seed; it wants to grow. Slowly you begin to move your arms, and then your body will begin to rise, straightening up until you are seated on your heels. Now you begin to lift your body up, and slowly, slowly you become erect, still kneeling on the ground.

The moment has come to break completely through the earth. You begin to rise slowly, placing one foot on the ground, then the other, fighting against the disequilibrium just as a shoot battles to make its own space, until finally you are standing. Imagine the area about you, the sun, the water, the wind, and the birds. Now you are a shoot that is beginning to grow. Slowly raise your arms toward the sky. Then stretch yourself more and more, more and more, as if you want to grasp the enormous sun that shines above you, giving you strength and attracting you. Your body begins to become more and more rigid, all of your muscles strain, and you feel yourself to be growing, growing, growing—you become huge. The tension increases more and more until it becomes painful, unbearable. When you can no longer stand it, scream and open your eyes.

Repeat this exercise for seven consecutive days, always at the same time.

river that ran in the distance. I arose slowly, with my eyes closed, and felt that at any moment I was going to become dizzy and fall to the ground. But meanwhile I continued to grow. My arms were spreading and my body stretching. There I was, being reborn, wanting to be bathed both inside and out by the immense sun that was shining and that was asking me to continue to grow more, stretch more, and embrace it with all of my branches. I was stretching my arms more and more, and the muscles throughout my body began to hurt. I felt that I was a thousand meters tall and that I could embrace mountains. And my body was expanding, expanding until the pain in my muscles became so intense that I couldn't bear it, and I screamed.

I opened my eyes, and Petrus was there in front of me, smiling and smoking a cigarette. The light of day had not yet disappeared, but I was surprised to see that the sun was not as bright as I had imagined. I asked if he wanted me to describe the sensations, and he said no.

"This is a very personal thing, and you should keep it to yourself. How can I judge it? The sensations are yours, not mine."

Petrus said that we were going to sleep right there. We built a small fire, drank what was left of his wine, and I made some sandwiches with a foie gras that I had bought before I reached Saint-Jean. Petrus went to the stream that ran nearby and caught some fish, which he fried over the fire. And then we crawled into our sleeping bags.

Among the greatest sensations that I have experienced in my life were those I felt on that unforgettable first night on the Road to Santiago. It was cold, despite its being summer, but I could still taste the warmth of the wine that Petrus had brought. I looked up at the sky; the Milky Way spread across it, reflecting the immensity of the Road we would have to travel. This immensity made me very anxious; it created a terrible fear that I would not be able to succeed—that I was too small for this task. Yet today I had been a seed and had been reborn. I had discovered that although the earth and my sleep were full of comfort, the life "up there" was much more beautiful. And I could always be reborn, as many times as I wanted, until my arms were long enough to embrace the earth from which I had come.

The Creator and the Created

(6)

For seven days we continued walking through the Pyrenees, climbing and descending the mountains, and each evening, as the rays of the sun reflected from the tallest peaks, Petrus had me perform the Seed Exercise. On the third day of our trek, we passed a cement marker, painted yellow, indicating that we had crossed the frontier; from then on we would be walking through Spain. Little by little, Petrus began to reveal some things about his private life; I learned that he was Italian and that he worked in industrial design.[1]

I asked him whether he was worried about the many things he had been forced to abandon in order to guide a pilgrim in search of his sword.

[1]It has been said that there is no such thing as coincidence in this world, and the following story confirms the truth of this assertion once again. One afternoon, I was leafing through some magazines in the lobby of the hotel where I was staying in Madrid, when I noticed a piece about the Prince of Asturias Prize; a Brazilian journalist, Roberto Marinho, had been one of the prize winners. A closer study of the photograph of those at the awards dinner startled me, though. At one of the tables, elegantly dressed in his tuxedo, was Petrus, described in the caption as "one of the most famous European designers of the moment."

"Let me explain something to you," he answered. "I am not guiding you to your sword. It is your job, solely and exclusively, to find it. I am here to lead you along the Road to Santiago and to teach you the RAM practices. How you apply this to your search for your sword is your problem."

"But you didn't answer my question."

"When you travel, you experience, in a very practical way, the act of rebirth. You confront completely new situations, the day passes more slowly, and on most journeys you don't even understand the language the people speak. So you are like a child just out of the womb. You begin to attach much more importance to the things around you because your survival depends upon them. You begin to be more accessible to others because they may be able to help you in difficult situations. And you accept any small favor from the gods with great delight, as if it were an episode you would remember for the rest of your life.

"At the same time, since all things are new, you see only the beauty in them, and you feel happy to be alive. That's why a religious pilgrimage has always been one of the most objective ways of achieving insight. The word *peccadillo*, which means a "small sin," comes from *pecus*, which means "defective foot," a foot that is incapable of walking a road. The way to correct the peccadillo is always to walk forward, adapting oneself to new situations and receiving in return all of the thousands of blessings that life generously offers to those who seek them.

"So why would you think that I might be worried about a half-dozen projects that I left behind in order to be here with you?"

Petrus looked around him, and I followed his eyes. On the uplands of one of the peaks, some goats were grazing. One of them, more daring than the others, stood on an outcropping of a high boulder, and I could not figure out how he had reached that spot or how he would get down. But as I was thinking this, the goat leapt and, alighting in a place I couldn't even see, rejoined his companions. Everything in our surroundings reflected an uneasy peace, the peace of a world that was still in the process of growing and being created—a world that seemed to know that, in order to grow, it had to continue moving along, always moving along. Great earthquakes and killer storms might make nature seem cruel, but I could see that these were just the vicissitudes of being on the road. Nature itself journeyed, seeking illumination.

"I am very glad to be here," said Petrus, "because the work I did not finish is not important and the work I will be able to do after I get back will be so much better."

When I had read the works of Carlos Castaneda, I had wanted very much to meet the old medicine man, Don Juan. Watching Petrus look at the mountains, I felt that I was with someone very much like him.

On the afternoon of the seventh day, after having passed through some pine woods, we reached the top of a mountain. There, Charlemagne had said his prayers for the first time on Spanish soil, and now an ancient monument urged in Latin that all who passed by should say a Salve Regina. We both did as the monument asked. Then Petrus had me do the Seed Exercise for the last time.

There was a strong wind, and it was cold. I argued that it was still early—at the latest, it was only three in the afternoon—but he told me not to talk about it, just do exactly as he ordered.

I knelt on the ground and began to perform the exercise. Everything went as usual until the moment when I extended my arms and began to imagine the sun. When I reached that point, with the gigantic sun shining there in front of me, I felt myself entering into a state of ecstasy. My memories of human life began slowly to dim, and I was no longer doing an exercise: I had become a tree. I was happy about this. The sun shone and revolved, which had never happened before. I remained there, my branches extended, my leaves trembling in the wind, not wanting ever to change my position—until something touched me, and everything went dark for a fraction of a second.

I immediately opened my eyes. Petrus had slapped me across the face and was holding me by the shoulders.

"Don't lose sight of your objective!" he said, enraged. "Don't forget that you still have a great deal to learn before you find your sword!"

I sat down on the ground, shivering in the cold wind.

"Does that always happen?" I asked.

"Almost always," he said. "Mainly with people like you, who are fascinated by details and forget what they are after."

Petrus took a sweater from his knapsack and put it on. I put my overshirt on, covering my "I LOVE NY" T-shirt. I would never have imagined that in "the hottest summer of the decade," according to the newspapers, it could be so cold. The two shirts helped to cut the wind, but I asked Petrus if we couldn't move along more quickly so that I could warm up.

The Road now made for an easy descent. I thought that the extreme cold I had experienced was due to the fact that we had eaten very frugally, just fish and the fruits of the forest.[2]

Petrus said that it wasn't the lack of food and explained that it was cold because we had reached the highest point in that range of mountains.

We had not gone more than five hundred meters when, at a curve in the Road, the scene changed completely. A

---

[2]There is a red fruit whose name I do not know, but just the sight of it today makes me nauseated from having eaten so much of it while walking through the Pyrenees.

tremendous, rolling plain extended into the distance. And to the left, on the Road down, less than two hundred meters away, a beautiful little village awaited us with its chimneys smoking.

I began to walk faster, but Petrus held me back.

"I think that this is a good time to teach you the second RAM practice," he said, sitting down on the ground and indicating that I should do the same.

I was irritated, but I did as he asked. The sight of the small village with its inviting chimney smoke had really upset me. Suddenly I realized that we had been out in the woods for a week; we had seen no one and had been either sleeping on the ground or walking throughout the day. I had run out of cigarettes, so I had been smoking the horrible roller tobacco that Petrus used. Sleeping in a sleeping bag and eating unseasoned fish were things that I had loved when I was twenty, but here on the Road to Santiago, they were sacrifices. I waited impatiently for Petrus to finish rolling his cigarette, while I thought about the warmth of a glass of wine in the bar I could see less than five minutes down the Road.

Petrus, bundled up in his sweater, was relaxed and looked out over the immense plain.

"What do you think about this crossing of the Pyrenees?" he asked, after a while.

"Very nice," I answered, not wanting to prolong the conversation.

"It must have been nice, because it took us six days to go a distance we could have gone in one."

I could not believe what he was saying. He pulled out the map and showed me the distance: seventeen kilometers. Even walking at a slow pace because of the ups and downs, the Road could have been hiked in six hours.

"You are so concerned about finding your sword that you forgot the most important thing: you have to get there.

Looking only for Santiago—which you can't see from here, in any case—you didn't see that we passed by certain places four or five times, approaching them from different angles."

Now that Petrus mentioned it, I began to realize that Mount Itchasheguy—the highest peak in the region—had sometimes been to my right and sometimes to my left. Although I had noticed this, I had not drawn the only possible conclusion: that we had gone back and forth many times.

"All I did was to follow different routes, using the paths made through the woods by the smugglers. But it was your responsibility to have seen that. This happened because the process of moving along did not exist for you. The only thing that existed was your desire to arrive at your goal."

"Well, what if I had noticed?"

"We would have taken seven days anyway, because that is what the RAM practices call for. But at least you would have approached the Pyrenees in a different way."

I was so surprised that I forgot about the village and the temperature.

"When you are moving toward an objective," said Petrus, "it is very important to pay attention to the road. It is the road that teaches us the best way to get there, and the road enriches us as we walk its length. You can compare it to a sexual relationship: the caresses of foreplay determine the intensity of the orgasm. Everyone knows that.

"And it is the same thing when you have an objective in your life. It will turn out to be better or worse depending on the route you choose to reach it and the way you negotiate that route. That's why the second RAM practice is so important; it extracts from what we are used to seeing every day the secrets that because of our routine, we never see."

And then Petrus taught me the Speed Exercise.

"In the city, amid all the things we have to do every day, this exercise should be done for twenty minutes. But since we

THE SPEED EXERCISE

Walk for twenty minutes at half the speed at which you normally walk. Pay attention to the details, people, and surroundings. The best time to do this is after lunch.

Repeat the exercise for seven days.

are on the Strange Road to Santiago, we should wait an hour before getting to the village."

The cold—about which I had already forgotten—returned, and I looked at Petrus with desperation. But he paid no attention; he got up, grabbed his knapsack, and began to walk the two hundred meters to the village with an exasperating slowness. At first, I looked only in the direction of the tavern, a small, ancient, two-story building with a wooden sign hanging above the door. We were so close that I could even read the year when the tavern had been built: 1652. We were moving, but it seemed as if we had not left our original spot. Petrus placed one foot in front of the other very slowly, and I did the same. I took my watch from my knapsack and strapped it on my wrist.

"It's going to be worse that way," he said, "because time isn't something that always proceeds at the same pace. It is we who determine how quickly time passes."

I began to look at my watch every minute and found that he was right. The more I looked at it, the more slowly the minutes passed. I decided to take his advice, and I put the watch back in my knapsack. I tried to pay more attention to the Road, the plain, and the stones I stepped on, but I kept looking ahead to the tavern—and I was convinced that we hadn't moved at all. I thought about telling myself some stories, but the exercise was making me anxious, and I couldn't concentrate. When I couldn't resist any longer and took my watch out again, only eleven minutes had passed.

"Don't make a torture out of this exercise, because it wasn't meant to be that," said Petrus. "Try to find pleasure in a speed that you're not used to. Changing the way you do routine things allows a new person to grow inside of you. But when all is said and done, you're the one who must decide how you handle it."

The kindness expressed in his final phrase calmed me down a bit. If it was I who decided what I would do, then it was better to take advantage of the situation. I breathed deeply and tried not to think. I put myself into a strange state, one in which time was something distant and of no interest to me. I calmed myself more and more and began to perceive the things that surrounded me through new eyes. My imagination, which was unavailable when I was tense, began to work to my advantage. I looked at the small village there in front of me and began to create a story about it: how it had been built, the pilgrims that had passed through it, the delight in finding people and lodging after the cold wind of the Pyrenees. At one point, I sensed that there was in the village a strong, mysterious, and all-knowing presence. My imagination peopled the plain with knights and battles. I could see their swords shining in the sun and hear the cries of war. The village was no longer just a place where I could warm my soul with wine and my body with a blanket; it was a historic monument, the work of heroic people who had left everything behind to become a part of that solitary place. The world was there around me, and I realized that seldom had I paid attention to it.

When I regained my everyday awareness, we were at the door of the tavern, and Petrus was inviting me to enter.

"I'll buy the wine," he said. "And let's get to sleep early, because tomorrow I have to introduce you to a great sorcerer."

Mine was a deep and dreamless sleep. As soon as daylight began to show itself in the two streets of the village of Roncesvalles, Petrus knocked on my door. We were in rooms on the top floor of the tavern, which also served as a hotel.

We had some coffee and some bread with olive oil, and we left, plodding through the dense fog that had fallen over the area. I could see that Roncesvalles wasn't exactly a village, as I had thought at first. At the time of the great pilgrimages along the Road, it had been the most powerful monastery in the region, with direct influence over the territory that extended all the way to the Navarra border. And it still retained some of its original character: its few buildings had been part of a religious brotherhood. The only construction that had any lay characteristics was the tavern where we had stayed.

We walked through the fog to the Collegiate Church. Inside, garbed in white, several monks were saying the first morning mass in unison. I couldn't understand a word they were saying, since the mass was being celebrated in Basque. Petrus sat in one of the pews to the side and indicated that I should join him.

The church was enormous and filled with art objects of incalculable value. Petrus explained to me in a whisper that it had been built through donations from the kings and queens of Portugal, Spain, France, and Germany, on a site selected by the emperor Charlemagne. On the high altar, the Virgin of Roncesvalles—sculpted in massive silver, with a face of precious stone—held in her hands a branch of flowers made of jewels. The smell of incense, the Gothic construction, and the chanting monks in white began to induce in me a state similar to the trances I had experienced during the rituals of the Tradition.

"And the sorcerer?" I asked, remembering what he had said on the previous afternoon.

Petrus indicated with a nod of his head a monk who was middle-aged, thin, and bespectacled, sitting with the other brothers on the narrow benches beside the high altar. A sorcerer, and at the same time a monk! I was eager for the mass to be over, but as Petrus had said to me the day before, it is we who determine the pace of time: my anxiety caused the religious ceremony to last for more than an hour.

When the mass was over, Petrus left me alone in the pew and went out through the door that the monks had used as an exit. I remained there for a while, gazing about the church and feeling that I should offer some kind of prayer, but I wasn't able to concentrate. The images appeared to be in the distance, locked in a past that would never return, like the Golden Age of the Road to Santiago.

Petrus appeared in the doorway and, without a word, signaled that I should follow him.

We came to an inside garden of the monastery, surrounded by a stone veranda. At the center of the garden there was a fountain, and seated at its edge, waiting for us, was the bespectacled monk.

"Father Jordi, this is the pilgrim," said Petrus, introducing me.

The monk held out his hand, and I shook it. No one said anything else. I was waiting for something to happen, but I heard only the crowing of roosters in the distance and the cries of the hawks taking off for their daily hunt. The monk looked at me expressionlessly, in a way that reminded me of Mme Lourdes's manner after I had spoken the Ancient Word.

Finally, after a long and uncomfortable silence, Father Jordi spoke.

"It looks to me like you rose through the levels of the Tradition a bit early, my friend."

I answered that I was thirty-eight and had been quite successful in all of the trials.[3]

---

[3]Trials are ritual tests in which importance is given not only to the disciple's dedication but also to the auguries that emerge during their execution. This usage of the term originated during the Inquisition.

"Except for one, the last and most important," he said, continuing to look at me without expression. "And without that one, nothing you have learned has any significance."

"That is why I am walking the Road to Santiago."

"Which guarantees nothing. Come with me."

Petrus stayed in the garden, and I followed Father Jordi. We crossed the cloisters, passed the place where a king was buried—Sancho the Strong—and went to a small chapel set among the group of main buildings that made up the monastery of Roncesvalles.

There was almost nothing inside: only a table, a book, and a sword—a sword that wasn't mine.

Father Jordi sat at the table, leaving me standing. He took some herbs and lit them, filling the place with their perfume. More and more, the situation reminded me of my encounter with Mme Lourdes.

"First, I want to tell you something," said Father Jordi. "The Jacobean route is only one of four roads. It is the Road of the Spades, and it may give you power, but that is not enough."

"What are the other three?"

"You know at least two others: the Road to Jerusalem, which is the Road of the Hearts, or of the Grail, and which endows you with the ability to perform miracles; and the Road to Rome, which is the Road of the Clubs; it allows you to communicate with other worlds."

"So what's missing is the Road of the Diamonds to complete the four suits of the deck," I joked. And the father laughed.

"Exactly. That's the secret Road. If you take it someday, you won't be helped by anybody. For now, let us leave that one aside. Where are your scallop shells?"

I opened my knapsack and took out the shells on which stood the image of Our Lady of the Visitation. He put the figure on the table. He held his hands over it and began to concentrate. He told me to do the same. The perfume in the air was growing stronger. Both the monk and I had our eyes open, and suddenly I could sense that the same phenomenon was occurring as had taken place at Itatiaia: the shells glowed with a light that did not illuminate. The brightness grew and grew, and I heard a mysterious voice, emanating from Father Jordi's throat, saying, "Wherever your treasure is, there will be your heart."

It was a phrase from the Bible. But the voice continued, "And wherever your heart is, there will be the cradle of the Second Coming of Christ; like these shells, the pilgrim is only an outer layer. When that layer, which is a stratum of life, is broken, life appears, and that life is comprised of agape."

He drew back his hands, and the shells lost their glow. Then he wrote my name in the book that was on the table. Along the Road to Santiago, I saw only three books where my name was written: Mme Lourdes's, Father Jordi's, and the Book of Power, where later I was to write my own name.

"That's all," he said. "You can go with the blessing of the Virgin of Roncesvalles and of San Tiago of the Sword.

"The Jacobean route is marked with yellow pointers, painted all the way across Spain," said the monk, as we returned to the place where Petrus was waiting. "If you should lose your way at any time, look for the markers—on trees, on stones, and on traffic signs—and you will be able to find a safe place."

"I have a good guide."

"But try to depend mainly on yourself—so that you aren't coming and going for six days in the Pyrenees."

So the monk already knew the story.

We found Petrus and then said good-bye. As we left Roncesvalles that morning, the fog had disappeared completely.

A straight, flat road extended in front of us, and I began to see the yellow markers Father Jordi had mentioned. The knapsack was a bit heavier, because I had bought a bottle of wine at the tavern, despite the fact that Petrus had told me that it was unnecessary. After Roncesvalles, hundreds of small villages dotted the route, and I was to sleep outdoors very seldom.

"Petrus, Father Jordi spoke about the Second Coming of Christ as if it were something that were happening now."

"It is always happening. That is the secret of your sword."

"And you told me that I was going to meet with a sorcerer, but I met with a monk. What does magic have to do with the Catholic Church?"

Petrus said just one word:

"Everything."

Cruelty

"Right there. That's the exact spot where love was murdered," said the old man, pointing to a small church built into the rocks.

We had walked for five days in a row, stopping only to eat and sleep. Petrus continued to be guarded about his private life but asked many questions about Brazil and about my work. He said that he really liked my country, because the image he knew best was that of Christ the Redeemer on Corcovado, standing open armed rather than suffering on the cross. He wanted to know everything, and he especially wanted to know if the women were as pretty as the ones here in Spain. The heat of the day was almost unbearable, and in all of the bars and villages where we stopped, the people complained about the drought. Because of the heat, we adopted the Spanish custom of the siesta and rested between two and four in the afternoon when the sun was at its hottest.

That afternoon, as we sat in an olive grove, the old man had come up to us and offered us a taste of wine. In spite of the heat, the habit of drinking wine had been part of life in that region for centuries.

"What do you mean, love was murdered there?" I asked, since the old man seemed to want to strike up a conversation.

"Many centuries ago, a princess who was walking the Road to Santiago, Felicia of Aquitaine, decided, on her way back from Compostela, to give up everything and live here. She was love itself, because she divided all of her wealth among the poor people of the region and began to care for the sick."

Petrus had lit one of his horrible rolled cigarettes, but despite his air of indifference, I could see that he was listening carefully to the old man's story.

"Her brother, Duke Guillermo, was sent by their father to bring her home. But Felicia refused to go. In desperation, the duke fatally stabbed her there in that small church that you can see in the distance; she had built it with her own hands in order to care for the poor and offer praise to God.

"When he came to his senses and realized what he had done, the duke went to Rome to ask the pope's forgiveness. As penitence, the pope ordered him to walk to Compostela. Then a curious thing happened: on his way back, when he arrived here, he had the same impulse as his sister, and he stayed on, living in that little church that his sister had built, caring for the poor until the last days of his long life."

"That's the law of retribution at work," Petrus laughed. The old man did not understand, but I knew what Petrus was saying. His concept of the law of retribution was similar to that of karma, or of the concept that as one sows, so shall they reap.

As we had been walking, we had gotten involved in some long theological discussions about the relationship between God and humanity. I had argued that in the Tradition, there was always an involvement with God, but that it was a complex one. The path to God, for me, was quite different from the one we were following on the Road to Santiago, with its

46

priests who were sorcerers, its gypsies who were devils, and its saints who performed miracles. All of these things seemed to me to be primitive, and too much connected with Christianity; they lacked the fascination, the elegance and the ecstasy that the rituals of the Tradition evoked in me. Petrus, on the other hand, argued that the guiding concept along the Road to Santiago was its simplicity. That the Road was one along which any person could walk, that its significance could be understood by even the least sophisticated person, and that, in fact, only such a road as that could lead to God. So Petrus thought my relationship to God was based too much on concept, on intellect and on reasoning; I felt that his was too simplistic and intuitive.

"You believe that God exists, and so do I," Petrus had said at one point. "So God exists for both of us. But if someone doesn't believe in him, that doesn't mean God ceases to exist. Nor does it mean that the nonbeliever is wrong."

"Does that mean that the existence of God depends on a person's desire and power?"

"I had a friend once who was drunk all the time but who said three Hail Marys every night. His mother had conditioned him to do so ever since he was a child. Even when he came home helplessly drunk, and even though he did not believe in God, my friend always said his three Hail Marys. After he died, I was at a ritual of the Tradition, and I asked the spirit of the ancients where my friend was. The spirit answered that he was fine and that he was surrounded by light. Without ever having had the faith during his life, the three prayers he had said ritualistically every day had brought him salvation.

"God was manifest in the caves and in the thunderstorms of prehistory. After people began to see God's hand in the caves and thunderstorms, they began to see him in the animals and in special places in the forest. During certain difficult times, God existed only in the catacombs of the great cities. But through all of time, he never ceased to live in the human heart in the form of love.

"In recent times, some thought that God was merely a concept, subject to scientific proof. But, at this point, history has been reversed, or rather is starting all over again. Faith and love have resumed their importance. When Father Jordi cited that quotation from Jesus, saying that wherever your treasure is, there also would your heart be, he was referring to the importance of love and good works. Wherever it is that you want to see the face of God, there you will see it. And if you don't want to see it, that doesn't matter, so long as you are performing good works. When Felicia of Aquitaine built her small church and began to help the poor, she forgot about the God of the Vatican. She became God's manifestation by becoming wiser and by living a simpler life—in other words, through love. It is in that respect that the old man was absolutely right in saying that love had been murdered."

Now Petrus said, "The law of retribution was operating when Felicia's brother felt forced to continue the good works he had interrupted. Anything is permissable but the interruption of a manifestation of love. When that happens, whoever tried to destroy it is responsible for its recreation."

I explained that in my country the law of return said that people's deformities and diseases were punishments for mistakes committed in previous incarnations.

"Nonsense," said Petrus. "God is not vengeance, God is love. His only form of punishment is to make someone who interrupts a work of love continue it."

The old man excused himself, saying that it was late and that he had to get back to work. Petrus thought it was a good time for us to get up, too, and get back on the Road.

"Let's forget all of our discussion about God," he said, as we made our way through the olive trees. "God is in everything around us. He has to be felt and lived. And here I am trying to transform him into a problem in logic so that you can understand him. Keep doing the exercise of walking slowly, and you will learn more and more about his presence."

Two days later, we had to climb a mountain called the Peak of Forgiveness. The climb took several hours, and at the top, I was shocked to find a group of tourists sunbathing and drinking beer; their car radios blasted music at top volume. They had driven up a nearby road to get to the top of the mountain.

"That's the way it is," said Petrus. "Did you expect that you were going to find one of El Cid's warriors up here, watching for the next Moorish attack?"

As we descended, I performed the Speed Exercise for the last time. Before us was another immense plain with sparse vegetation burned by the drought; it was bordered by blue mountains. There were almost no trees, only the rocky ground and some cactus. At the end of the exercise, Petrus asked me about my work, and it was only then that I realized that I hadn't thought about it for some time. My worries about business and about the things I had left undone had practically disappeared. Now I thought of these things only at night, and even then I didn't give them much importance. I was happy to be there, walking the Road to Santiago.

I told Petrus how I was feeling, and he joked, "Any time now you are going to do the same thing as Felicia of Aquitaine." Then he stopped and asked me to put my knapsack on the ground.

"Look around you, and choose some point to fixate on," he said.

I chose the cross on a church that I could see in the distance.

"Keep your eyes fixed on that point, and try to concentrate only on what I am going to tell you. Even if you feel something different, don't become distracted. Do as I am telling you."

I stood there, relaxed, with my eyes fixed on the cross, as Petrus took a position behind me and pressed a finger into the base of my neck.

"The Road you are traveling is the Road of power, and only the exercises having to do with power will be taught to you. The journey, which prior to this was torture because all you wanted to do was get there, is now beginning to become a pleasure. It is the pleasure of searching and the pleasure of an adventure. You are nourishing something that's very important—your dreams.

"We must never stop dreaming. Dreams provide nourishment for the soul, just as a meal does for the body. Many times in our lives we see our dreams shattered and our desires frustrated, but we have to continue dreaming. If we don't, our soul dies, and agape cannot reach it. A lot of blood has been shed in those fields out there; some of the cruelest battles of Spain's war to expel the Moors were fought on them. Who was in the right or who knew the truth does not matter; what's important is knowing that both sides were fighting the good fight.

"The good fight is the one we fight because our heart asks it of us. In the heroic ages—at the time of the knights in armor—this was easy. There were lands to conquer and much to do. Today, though, the world has changed a lot, and the good fight has shifted from the battlefields to the fields within ourselves.

"The good fight is the one that's fought in the name of our dreams. When we're young and our dreams first explode inside us with all of their force, we are very courageous, but we haven't yet learned how to fight. With great effort, we learn how to fight, but by then we no longer have the courage to go into combat. So we turn against ourselves and do battle within. We become our own worst enemy. We say that our dreams were childish, or too difficult to realize, or the result of our not having known enough about life. We kill our dreams because we are afraid to fight the good fight."

The pressure of Petrus's finger on my neck became stronger. I perceived that the cross on the church had been transformed; now its outline seemed to be that of a winged being, an angel. I blinked my eyes, and the cross became a cross again.

"The first symptom of the process of our killing our dreams is the lack of time," Petrus continued. "The busiest people I have known in my life always have time enough to do everything. Those who do nothing are always tired and pay no attention to the little amount of work they are required to do. They complain constantly that the day is too short. The truth is, they are afraid to fight the good fight.

"The second symptom of the death of our dreams lies in our certainties. Because we don't want to see life as a grand adventure, we begin to think of ourselves as wise and fair and correct in asking so little of life. We look beyond the walls of our day-to-day existence, and we hear the sound of lances breaking, we smell the dust and the sweat, and we see the great defeats and the fire in the eyes of the warriors. But we never see the delight, the immense delight in the hearts of those who are engaged in the battle. For them, neither victory nor defeat is important; what's important is only that they are fighting the good fight.

"And, finally, the third symptom of the passing of our dreams is peace. Life becomes a Sunday afternoon; we ask for nothing grand, and we cease to demand anything more than we are willing to give. In that state, we think of ourselves as being mature; we put aside the fantasies of our youth, and we seek personal and professional achievement. We are surprised when people our age say that they still want this or that out of life. But really, deep in our hearts, we know that what has happened is that we have renounced the battle for our dreams—we have refused to fight the good fight."

The tower of the church kept changing; now it appeared to be an angel with its wings spread. The more I blinked, the longer the figure remained. I wanted to speak to Petrus, but I sensed that he hadn't finished.

"When we renounce our dreams and find peace," he said after a while, "we go through a short period of tranquillity. But the dead dreams begin to rot within us and to infect our entire being. We become cruel to those around us, and then we begin to direct this cruelty against ourselves. That's when illnesses and psychoses arise. What we sought to avoid in combat—disappointment and defeat—come upon us because of our cowardice. And one day, the dead, spoiled dreams make it difficult to breathe, and we actually seek death. It's death that frees us from our certainties, from our work, and from that terrible peace of our Sunday afternoons."

Now I was sure that I was really seeing an angel, and I couldn't pay attention to what Petrus was saying. He must have sensed this, because he removed his finger from my neck and stopped talking. The image of the angel remained for a few moments and then disappeared. In its place, the tower of the church returned.

We were silent for a few minutes. Petrus rolled himself a cigarette and began to smoke. I took the bottle of wine from my knapsack and had a swallow. It was warm, but it was still delicious.

"What did you see?" he asked me.

I told him about the angel. I said that at the beginning, the image would disappear when I blinked.

"You, too, have to learn how to fight the good fight. You have already learned to accept the adventures and challenges that life provides, but you still want to deny anything that is extraordinary."

Petrus took a small object from his knapsack and handed it to me. It was a golden pin.

"This was a present from my grandmother. In the Order of RAM, all of the ancients have an object such as this. It's called "the Point of Cruelty." When you saw the angel appear on the church tower, you wanted to deny it, because it wasn't something that you are used to. In your view of the world, churches are churches, and visions occur only during the ecstasy created by the rituals of the Tradition."

I said that my vision must have been caused by the pressure he was applying to my neck.

"That's right, but that doesn't change anything. The fact is that you rejected the vision. Felicia of Aquitaine must have seen something similar, and she bet her entire life on what she saw. And the result of her having done that transformed her work into a work of love. The same thing probably happened to her brother. And the same thing happens to everyone every day: we always know which is the best road to follow, but we follow only the road that we have become accustomed to."

Petrus began to walk again, and I followed along. The rays of the sun made the pin in my hand glisten.

"The only way we can rescue our dreams is by being generous with ourselves. Any attempt to inflict self-punishment— no matter how subtle it may be—should be dealt with rigorously. In order to know when we are being cruel to ourselves, we have to transform any attempt at causing spiritual pain—such as guilt, remorse, indecision, and cowardice—into physical pain. By transforming a spiritual pain into a physical one, we can learn what harm it can cause us."

And then Petrus taught me the Cruelty Exercise.

THE CRUELTY EXERCISE

Every time a thought comes to mind that makes you feel bad about yourself—jealousy, self-pity, envy, hatred, and so on—do the following:

Dig the nail of your index finger into the cuticle of the thumb of the same hand until it becomes quite painful. Concentrate on the pain: it is a physical reflection of the suffering you are going through spiritually. Ease the pressure only when the cruel thought has gone.

Repeat this as many times as necessary until the thought has left you, even if this means digging your fingernail into your thumb over and over. Each time, it will take longer for the cruel thought to return, and eventually it will disappear altogether, so long as you do not fail to perform the exercise every time it comes to mind.

"In ancient times, they used a golden pin for this," he said. "Nowadays, things have changed, just as the sights along the Road to Santiago change."

Petrus was right. Seen from down at this level, the plain appeared to be a series of mountains in front of me.

"Think of something cruel that you did to yourself today, and perform the exercise."

I couldn't think of anything.

"That's the way it always is. We are only able to be kind to ourselves at the few times when we need severity."

Suddenly I remembered that I had called myself an idiot for having laboriously climbed the Peak of Forgiveness while the tourists had driven up in their cars. I knew that this was unfair and that I had been cruel to myself; the tourists, after all, were only looking for a place to sunbathe, while I was looking for my sword. I wasn't an idiot, even if I had felt like one. I dug the nail of my index finger forcefully into the cuticle of my thumb. I felt intense pain, and as I concentrated on it, the feeling of having been an idiot dissipated.

I described this to Petrus, and he laughed without saying anything.

That night, we stayed in a comfortable hotel in the village where the church I had focused on was located. After dinner, we decided to take a walk through the streets, as an aid to digestion.

"Of all the ways we have found to hurt ourselves, the worst has been through love. We are always suffering because of someone who doesn't love us, or someone who has left us, or someone who won't leave us. If we are alone, it is because no one wants us; if we are married, we transform the marriage into slavery. What a terrible thing!" he said angrily.

We came to a square, and there was the church I had seen. It was small and lacked any architectural distinction. Its bell tower reached up toward the sky. I tried to see the angel again, but I couldn't.

"When the Son of God descended to earth, he brought love to us. But since people identified love only with suffering and sacrifice, they felt they had to crucify Jesus. Had they not done so, no one would have believed in the love that Jesus brought, since people were so used to suffering every day with their own problems."

We sat on the curb and stared at the church. Once again, it was Petrus who broke the silence.

"Do you know what Barabbas means, Paulo? *Bar* means son, and *abba* means father."

He gazed at the cross on the bell tower. His eyes shone, and I sensed that he was moved by something—perhaps by the love he had spoken so much about, but I couldn't be certain.

"The intentions of the divine glory were so wise!" he said, his voice echoing in the empty square. "When Pontius Pilate made the people choose, he actually gave them no choice at all. He presented them with one man who had been whipped and was falling apart, and he presented them with another man who held his head high—Barabbas, the revolutionary. God knew that the people would put the weaker one to death so that he could prove his love."

He concluded, "And regardless of which choice they made, it was the Son of God who was going to be crucified."

The Messenger

And here all Roads to Santiago become one."

It was early in the morning when we reached Puente de la Reina, where the name of the village was etched into the base of a statue of a pilgrim in medieval garb: three-cornered hat, cape, scallop shells, and in his hand a shepherd's crook with a gourd—a memorial to the epic journey, now almost forgotten, that Petrus and I were reliving.

We had spent the previous night at one of the many monasteries along the Road. The brother of the gate who had greeted us had warned us that we were not to speak a word within the walls of the abbey. A young monk had led each of us to an alcove, furnished only with the bare necessities: a hard bed, old but clean sheets, a pitcher of water and a basin for personal hygiene. There was no plumbing or hot water, and the schedule for meals was posted behind the door.

At the time indicated, we had come down to the dining hall. Because of the vow of silence, the monks communicated only with their glances, and I had the impression that their eyes gleamed with more intensity than those of other people. The supper was served early at narrow tables where we sat with the monks in their brown habits. From his seat, Petrus had given me a signal, and I had understood perfectly what he meant: he was dying to light a cigarette, but it looked like he was going to have to go through the entire night without one. The same was true for me, and I dug a nail into the cuticle of my thumb, which was already like raw meat. The moment was too beautiful for me to commit any kind of cruelty toward myself.

The meal was served: vegetable soup, bread, fish, and wine. Everyone prayed, and we recited the invocation with them. Afterward, as we ate, a monk read from an Epistle of Saint Paul.

"But God hath chosen the foolish things of the world to put to shame the wise, and God hath chosen the weak things of the world to put to shame the things which are mighty," read the monk in a thin, tuneless voice. "We are fools for Christ's sake. We are made as the filth of the world and are the offscouring of all things unto this day. But the kingdom of God is not in word but in power."

The admonitions of Paul to the Corinthians echoed off the bare walls of the dining hall throughout the meal.

As we entered Puente de la Reina we had been talking about the monks of the previous night. I confessed to Petrus that I had smoked in my room, in mortal fear that someone would smell my cigarette burning. He laughed, and I could tell that he had probably done the same thing.

"Saint John the Baptist went into the desert, but Jesus went among the sinners, and he traveled endlessly," Petrus said. "That's my preference, too."

In fact, aside from the time he had spent in the desert, Jesus had spent all of his life among people.

"Actually, his first miracle was not the saving of someone's soul nor the curing of a disease, and it wasn't an expulsion of the devil; it was the transformation of water into an excellent wine at a wedding because the wine supply of the owner of the house had run out."

After Petrus said this, he suddenly stopped walking. It was so abrupt that I became alarmed and stopped, too. We were at the bridge that gave its name to the village. Petrus, though, wasn't looking at the road in front of us. His eyes were fastened on two boys who were playing with a rubber ball at the edge of the river. They were eight or ten years old and seemed not to have noticed us. Instead of crossing the bridge, Petrus scrambled down the bank and approached the two boys. As always, I followed him without question.

The boys continued to ignore us. Petrus sat down to watch them at play, until the ball fell close to where he was seated. With a quick movement, he grabbed the ball and threw it to me.

I caught the ball in the air and waited to see what would happen.

One of the boys—the elder of the two—approached me. My first impulse was to throw him the ball, but Petrus's behavior had been so unusual that I decided that I would try to understand what was happening.

"Give me the ball, Mister," said the boy.

I looked at the small figure two meters away from me. I sensed that there was something familiar about him. It was the same feeling I had had about the gypsy.

The lad asked for the ball several times, and when he got no response from me, he bent down and picked up a stone.

"Give me the ball, or I'll throw a stone at you," he said.

Petrus and the other boy were watching me silently. The boy's aggressiveness irritated me.

"Throw the stone," I answered. "If it hits me, I'll come over there and whack you one."

I sensed that Petrus gave a sigh of relief. Something in the back of my mind told me that I had already lived through this scene.

The boy was frightened by what I said. He let the stone fall and tried a different approach.

"There's a relic here in Puente de la Reina. It used to belong to a rich pilgrim. I see by your shell and your knapsack that you are pilgrims. If you give me my ball, I'll give you the relic. It's hidden in the sand here along the river."

"I want to keep the ball," I answered, without much conviction. Actually, I wanted the relic. The boy seemed to be telling the truth. But maybe Petrus needed the ball for some reason, and I didn't want to disappoint him. He was my guide.

"Look, Mister, you don't need the ball," the boy said, now with tears in his eyes. "You're strong, and you've been around, and you know the world. All I know is the edge of this river, and that ball is my only toy. Please give it back."

The boy's words got to me. But the strangely familiar surroundings and my feeling that I had already read about or lived through the situation made me refuse again.

"No. I need the ball. I'll give you enough money to buy another one, even better than this one, but this one is mine."

When I said that, time seemed to stop. The surroundings began to change, even without Petrus's finger at my neck; for a fraction of a second, it seemed that we had been transported to a broad, terrifying, ashen desert. Neither Petrus nor the other boy was there, just myself and the boy in front of me. He was older, and his features were kinder and friendlier. But there was a light in his eyes that frightened me.

The vision didn't last more than a second. Then I was back at Puente de la Reina, where the many Roads to Santiago, coming from all over Europe, became one. There in front of me, a boy was asking for his ball, with a sweet, sad look in his eye.

Petrus approached me, took the ball from my hand, and gave it to the boy.

"Where is the relic hidden?" he asked the boy.

"What relic?" he said, as he grabbed his friend's hand, jumped away, and threw himself into the water.

We climbed the bank and crossed the bridge. I began to ask questions about what had happened, and I described my vision of the desert, but Petrus changed the subject and said that we should talk about it when we had traveled further from that spot.

Half an hour later, we came to a stretch of the Road that still showed vestiges of Roman paving. Here was another bridge, this one in ruins, and we sat down to have the breakfast that had been given to us by the monks: rye bread, yogurt, and goat's cheese.

"Why did you want the kid's ball?" Petrus asked me.

I told him that I hadn't wanted the ball—that I had acted that way because Petrus himself had behaved so strangely, as if the ball were very important to him.

"In fact, it was. It allowed you to win out over your personal devil."

My personal devil? This was the most ridiculous thing I had heard during the entire trip. I had spent six days coming and going in the Pyrenees, I had met a sorcerer priest who had performed no sorcery, and my finger was raw meat because every time I had a cruel thought about myself—from hypochondria, to feelings of guilt, to an inferiority complex—I had to dig my fingernail into my wounded thumb. But about one thing Petrus was right: my negative thinking had diminished considerably. Still, this story about having a personal devil was something I had never heard—and I wasn't going to swallow it easily.

"Today, before crossing the bridge, I had a strong feeling of the presence of someone, someone who was trying to give us a warning. But the warning was more for you than for me. A battle is coming on very soon, and you will have to fight the good fight.

"When you do not know your personal devil, he usually manifests himself in the nearest person. I looked around, and I saw those boys playing—and I figured that it was there that he would probably give his warning. But I was only following a hunch. I became sure that it was your personal devil when you refused to give the ball back."

I repeated that I had done so because I thought it was what Petrus wanted.

"Why me? I never said a word."

I began to feel a little dizzy. Maybe it was the food, which I was devouring voraciously after almost an hour of walking and feeling hungry. Still, I could not escape the feeling that the boy had seemed familiar.

"Your personal devil tried three classical approaches: a threat, a promise, and an attack on your weak side. Congratulations: you resisted bravely."

Now I remembered that Petrus had asked the boy about the relic. At the time, I had thought that the boy's response showed that he had tried to fool me. But he must really have had a relic hidden there—a devil never makes false promises.

"When the boy could not remember about the relic, your personal devil had gone away."

Then he added without blinking, "It is time to call him back. You are going to need him."

We were sitting on the ruins of the old bridge. Petrus carefully gathered the remains of the meal and put them into the paper bag that the monks had given us. In the fields in front of us, the workers began to arrive for the day's plowing, but they were so far away that I couldn't hear what they were saying. It was rolling land, and the cultivated patches created unusual designs across the landscape. Under our feet, the water course, almost nonexistent due to the drought, made very little noise.

"Before he went out into the world, Christ went into the desert to talk with his personal devil," Petrus began. "He learned what he needed to know about people, but he did not let the devil dictate the rules of the game; that is how he won.

"Once, a poet said that no man is an island. In order to fight the good fight, we need help. We need friends, and when the friends aren't nearby, we have to turn solitude into our main weapon. We need the help of everything around us in order to take the necessary steps toward our goal. Everything has to be a personal manifestation of our will to win the good fight. If we don't understand that, then we don't recognize that we need everything and everybody, and we become arrogant warriors. And our arrogance will defeat us in the end, because we will be so sure of ourselves that we won't see the pitfalls there on the field of battle."

His comments about warriors and battles reminded me again of Carlos Castaneda's Don Juan. I asked myself whether the old medicine man would have given lessons early in the morning, before his disciple had even been able to digest his breakfast. But Petrus continued:

"Over and above the physical forces that surround us and help us, there are basically two spiritual forces on our side: an angel and a devil. The angel always protects us and is a divine gift—you do not have to invoke him. Your angel's face is always visible when you look at the world with eyes that are receptive. He is this river, the workers in the field, and that blue sky. This old bridge that helps us to cross the stream was built here by the hands of anonymous Roman legionnaires, and the bridge, too, is the face of your angel. Our grandparents called him the guardian angel.

"The devil is an angel, too, but he is a free, rebellious force. I prefer to call him the messenger, since he is the main link between you and the world. In antiquity, he was represented by Mercury and by Hermes Trismegistus, the messenger of the gods. His arena is only on the material plane. He is present in the gold of the Church, because the gold comes from the earth, and the earth is your devil. He is present in our work and in our ways of dealing with money. When we let him loose, his tendency is to disperse himself. When we exorcise him, we lose all of the good things that he has to teach us; he knows a great deal about the world and about human beings. When we become fascinated by his power, he owns us and keeps us from fighting the good fight.

"So the only way to deal with our messenger is to accept him as a friend—by listening to his advice and asking for his help when necessary, but never allowing him to dictate the rules of the game. Like you did with the boy. To keep the messenger from dictating the rules of the game, it is necessary first that you know what you want and then that you know his face and his name."

"How can I know them?" I asked.

And then Petrus taught me the Messenger Ritual.

"Wait until night to perform it, when it is easier," Petrus said. "Today, at your first meeting, he will tell you his name. This name is secret and should never be told to anyone, not even me. Whoever knows the name of your messenger can destroy you."

Petrus got up, and we began to walk. Shortly, we reached the field where the farmers were working. We said *"Buenos días"* to them and went on down the road.

"If I had to use a metaphor, I would say that your angel is your armor, and your messenger is your sword. Armor protects you under any set of circumstances, but a sword can fall to the ground in the midst of a battle, or it can kill a friend, or be turned against its owner. A sword can be used for almost anything . . . except as something to sit on," he said, laughing.

We stopped in a town for lunch, and the young waiter who served us was clearly in a bad mood. He didn't answer any of our questions, he served the meal sloppily, and he even succeeded in spilling coffee on Petrus's shorts. I watched my guide go through a transformation: furious, he went to find the owner and complained loudly about the waiter's rudeness. He wound up going to the men's room and taking off his shorts; the owner cleaned them and spread them out to dry.

As we waited for the two o'clock sun to dry Petrus's shorts, I was thinking about everything we had talked about that morning. It was true that most of what Petrus had said about the boy by the river made sense. After all, I had had a vision of the desert and of a face. But that story about "the messenger" seemed a little primitive to me. For a person with any intelligence here in the the twentieth century, the concepts of hell, of sin, and of the devil did not make much sense. In the Tradition, whose teachings I had followed for much longer than I had followed the Road to Santiago, the messenger was a spirit that ruled the forces of the earth and was always a friend. He was often used in magical operations but never as an ally or counselor with regard to daily events. Petrus had led me to believe that I could use the friendship of the messenger as a means to improve my work and my dealings with the world. Beside being profane, this idea seemed to me to be childish.

THE MESSENGER RITUAL

1. Sit down and relax completely. Let your mind wander and your thinking flow without restraint. After a while, begin to repeat to yourself, "Now I am relaxed, and I am in the deepest kind of sleep."

2. When you feel that your mind is no longer concerned with anything, imagine a billow of fire to your right. Make the flames lively and brilliant. Then quietly say, "I order my subconscious to show itself. I order it to open and reveal its magic secrets." Wait a bit, and concentrate only on the fire. If an image appears, it will be a manifestation of your subconscious. Try to keep it alive.

3. Keeping the fire always to your right, now begin to imagine another billow of fire to your left. When the flames are lively, say the following words quietly: "May the power of the Lamb, which manifests itself in everything and everyone, manifest itself also in me when I invoke my messenger. (Name of messenger) will appear before me now."

4. Talk with your messenger, who should appear between the two fires. Discuss your specific problems, ask for advice, and give him the necessary orders.

5. When your conversation has ended, dismiss the messenger with the following words: "I thank the Lamb for the miracle I have performed. May (name of messenger) return whenever he is invoked, and when he is far away, may he help me to carry on my work."

Note: On the first invocation—or during the first invocations, depending on the ability of the person performing the ritual to concentrate—do not say the name of the messenger. Just say "he." If the ritual is well performed, the messenger should immediately reveal his name telepathically. If not, insist until you learn his name, and only then begin the conversation. The more the ritual is repeated, the stronger the presence of the messenger will be and the more rapid his actions.

But I had sworn to Mme Lourdes that I would give total obedience to my guide. Once again, I had to dig my nail into my red, raw thumb.

"I should not have put him down," Petrus said about the waiter after we had left. "I mean, after all, he didn't spill that coffee on me but on the world that he hated. He knows that there is a huge world out there that extends well beyond the borders of his imagination. And his participation in that world is limited to getting up early, going to the bakery, waiting on whoever comes by, and masturbating every night, dreaming about the women he will never get to know."

It was the time of day when we usually stopped for our siesta, but Petrus had decided to keep walking. He said that it was a way of doing penance for his intolerance. And I, who had not done a thing, had to trudge along with him under the hot sun. I was thinking about the good fight and the millions of souls who, right then, were scattered all over the planet, doing things they didn't want to do. The Cruelty Exercise, in spite of having made my thumb raw, was helping me. It had helped me to see how my mind could betray me, pushing me into situations I wanted no part of and into feelings that were no help to me. Right then, I began to hope that Petrus was right: that a messenger really did exist and that I could talk to him about practical matters and ask him for help with my day-to-day problems. I was anxious for night to fall.

Meanwhile, Petrus could not stop talking about the waiter. Finally, he wound up convincing himself that he had acted properly; once again, he used a Christian argument to make his case.

"Christ forgave the adulterous woman but cursed the grower who would not give him a fig. And I am not here, either, just to be a nice guy."

That was it. In his view, the matter was settled. Once again, the Bible had saved him.

We reached Estella at almost nine o'clock at night. I took a bath, and we went down to eat. The author of the first guide for the Jacobean route, Aymeric Picaud, had described Estella as a "fertile place, with good bread and great wine, meat, and fish. Its river, the Ega, has good, fresh, clean water." I didn't drink the river water, but as far as the menu at our restaurant was concerned, Picaud's assessment was still right, even after eight centuries. It offered braised leg of lamb, artichoke hearts, and a Rioja wine from a very good year. We sat at the table for a long time, talking about inconsequential things and enjoying the wine. But finally Petrus said that it was a good time for me to have my first contact with my messenger.

We went out to look around the city. Some alleys led directly to the river—as they do in Venice—and I decided to sit down in one of them. Petrus knew that from that point on it was I who would conduct the ceremony, so he hung back.

I looked at the river for a long time. Its water and its sound began to take me out of this world and to create a profound serenity in me. I closed my eyes and imagined the first billow of fire. It was not easy to imagine at first, but finally it appeared.

I pronounced the ritual words, and another billow of fire appeared to my left. The space between the two billows, illuminated by the fires, was completely empty. I kept looking at that space for a while, trying not to think, so that the messenger would manifest himself. But instead of his appearing, various exotic scenes began to appear—the entrance to a pyramid, a woman dressed in pure gold, some black men dancing around a fire. The images came and went in rapid succession, and I let them flow uncontrolled. There also appeared some stretches of the Road that I had traversed with Petrus—byways, restaurants, forests—until, with no warning, the ashen desert that I had seen that morning appeared between the two fires. And there, looking at me, was the friendly man with the traitorous look in his eyes.

He laughed, and I smiled in my trance. He showed me a closed bag, then opened it and looked inside—but in such a way that I could not see into it. Then a name came to my mind: Astrain.[1]

I began to envision the name and make it dance between the two fires, and the messenger gave a nod of approval; I had learned his name.

It was time to end the exercise. I said the ritual words and extinguished the fires—first on the left and then on the right. I opened my eyes, and there was the river Ega in front of me.

"It was much less difficult than I had imagined," I said to Petrus, after I had told him about everything that had occurred between the two fires.

"This was your first contact—a meeting to establish mutual recognition and mutual friendship. Your conversations with the messenger will be productive if you invoke him every day and discuss your problems with him. But you have to know how to distinguish between what is real assistance and what is a trap. Keep your sword ready every time you meet with him."

"But I don't have my sword yet," I answered.

"Right, so he can't cause you much damage. But even so, don't make it easy for him."

---

[1]This is not the real name.

The ritual having ended, I left Petrus and went back to the hotel. In bed, I thought about the poor young waiter who had served us lunch. I felt like going back there and teaching him the Messenger Ritual, telling him that he could change everything if he wanted to. But it was useless to try to save the world: I hadn't even been able to save myself yet.[2]

[2]This description of my first experience with the Messenger Ritual is incomplete. Actually, Petrus explained the meaning of the visions, of the memories, and of the bag that Astrain showed me. But since each meeting with the messenger is different for every person, I do not want to insist on my own personal experience as it might influence the experience of others.

Love

Talking with your messenger doesn't mean asking questions about the world of the spirits," Petrus said the next day. "The messenger performs only one function for you: he helps you with regard to the material world. And he will give you this help only if you know exactly what it is that you want."

We had stopped in a town to have something to drink. Petrus had ordered a beer, and I asked for a soft drink. My fingers made abstract designs in the water on the table, and I was worried.

"You told me that the messenger had manifested himself in the boy because he needed to tell me something."

"Something urgent," he confirmed.

We talked some more about messengers, angels, and devils. It was difficult for me to accept such a practical application of the mysteries of the Tradition. Petrus said that we are always seeking some kind of reward. But I reminded him that Jesus had said that the rich man would not enter into the kingdom of heaven.

"But Jesus rewarded the man who knew how to make his master more adept. People did not believe in Jesus just because he was an outstanding orator: he had to perform miracles and reward those who followed him."

"No one is going to blaspheme Jesus in my bar," said the owner, who had been listening to our conversation.

"No one is blaspheming Jesus," Petrus answered. "People speak poorly of Jesus when they commit the sin of taking his name in vain. Like all of you did out there in the plaza."

The owner hesitated for a moment. But then he answered, "I had nothing to do with that. I was only a child at the time."

"The guilty ones are always the others," Petrus mumbled. The owner went into the kitchen, and I asked Petrus what he was talking about.

"Fifty years ago, in this twentieth century of ours, a gypsy was burned at the stake out there in the plaza. He was accused of sorcery and of blaspheming the sacred host. The case was lost amid the news of the Spanish civil war, and no one remembers it today. Except the people who live here."

"How do you know about it, Petrus?"

"Because I have already walked the Road to Santiago."

We went on drinking there in the empty bar. The sun was hot, and it was our siesta time. A few minutes later, the owner reappeared, accompanied by the town priest.

"Who are you people?" asked the priest.

Petrus showed him the scallop shells sewn to his knapsack. For twelve hundred years, pilgrims had passed along the Road in front of the bar, and the tradition was that every pilgrim was respected and welcomed under any circumstance. The priest changed his tone.

"How can it be that pilgrims on the Road to Santiago are speaking poorly of Jesus?" he asked, in a tone that was appropriate to a catechism.

74

"Nobody here was speaking poorly of Jesus. We were speaking poorly of the crimes committed in the name of Jesus. Like the gypsy that was burned at the stake there in the square."

The shells on Petrus's knapsack had also changed the owner's attitude. Now he addressed us with some respect.

"The curse of the gypsy is still with us today," he said, and the priest looked at him reprovingly.

Petrus wanted to know how. The priest said that these were stories told by the villagers and that the church did not approve of them. But the owner of the bar went on:

"Before the gypsy died, he said that the youngest child in the village was going to receive and incorporate his devils. And that when that child became old and died, the devils would pass on to another child. And so on, for all the centuries to come."

"The soil here is the same as the soil in the other towns around here," said the priest. "When the other towns have a drought, we do, too. When it rains and there's a good harvest, we fill our barns, too. Nothing has happened here with us that has not happened in the neighboring towns, too. This whole story is a fantasy."

"Nothing has happened because we isolated the curse," said the owner.

"Well, then, let's see it," answered Petrus. The priest laughed and said that that was no way to talk. The owner of the bar made the sign of the cross. But neither of them moved.

Petrus got the check and insisted that someone take us to the person who had inherited the curse. The priest excused himself, saying that he had been interrupted at something important and had to get back to his church. And he left before anyone could say anything.

The owner of the bar looked at Petrus fearfully.

"Not to worry," said my guide. "Just show us the house where the curse resides. We are going to try to rid the town of it."

The owner of the bar went out into the dusty street with us. The hot sun of the afternoon beat down everywhere. We walked to the outskirts of the town, and he pointed to a house set off by itself at the side of the Road.

"We always send meals, clothing, everything they need," he apologized. "But not even the priest goes in there."

We said good-bye to him and walked toward the house. The owner of the bar waited there, perhaps thinking that we would pass it by. But Petrus went up to the house and knocked on the door, and when I looked around, the bar owner had disappeared.

A woman of about seventy came to the door. At her side was an enormous black dog, wagging his tail and apparently happy to see company. The woman asked what we wanted; she said she was busy washing clothes and had left some pots on the fire. She did not seem surprised by our visit. I figured that many pilgrims, not knowing about the curse, must have knocked on the door seeking shelter.

"We are pilgrims on the Road to Compostela, and we need some hot water," Petrus said. "I knew that you would not refuse us."

With a show of irritation, the woman opened the door. We went into a small room, clean but poorly furnished. There was a sofa with its stuffing coming out, a bureau, and a Formica-topped table with two chairs. On the bureau was an image of the Sacred Heart of Jesus, some saints, and a crucifix made of mirrors. Through one of the two doors in the room, I could see the bedroom. The woman led Petrus through the other door into the kitchen.

"I have some water boiling," she said. "Let me get you a container, and you can both get going."

I was there in the living room, alone with the huge dog. He wagged his tail, docile and contented. The woman came back with an old can, filled it with water, and held it out to Petrus.

"There. Go with God's blessing."

But Petrus did not move. He took a tea bag from his knapsack, put it in the can, and said that he would like to share the little he had with her in appreciation for her welcome.

The woman, clearly upset now, brought two cups and sat down at the table with Petrus. I kept looking at the dog as I listened to their conversation.

"They told me in the village that there was a curse on this house," Petrus commented boldly. The dog's eyes seemed to light up, as if he had understood what had been said. The old woman stood up immediately.

"That's a lie. It's an old superstition. Please finish your tea, because I have lots of things to do."

The dog sensed the woman's sudden mood change. He remained still but alert. But Petrus continued to do what he was doing. He slowly poured the tea into the cup, raised it to his lips, and put it down on the table without drinking a drop.

"That's really hot," he said. "I think I will wait until it cools off a bit."

The woman did not sit down again. She was visibly uncomfortable with us there and clearly regretted having opened the door. She noticed that I was staring fixedly at the dog and called him to her. The animal obeyed, but when he reached her side, he turned to look at me.

"This is why he did it, my friend," Petrus said, looking at me. "This is why your messenger appeared yesterday in the child."

Suddenly I realized that I was not just looking at the dog. As soon as I had come in, the animal had hypnotized me and had kept my eyes fastened on him. The dog was staring at me and making me do as he wanted. I began to feel weak, as if I would like to lie down and sleep on the torn couch; it was really hot outside, and I did not feel much like walking. The feelings all seemed strange to me, and I had the impression that I was falling into a trap. The dog continued to look fixedly at me, and the more he looked at me, the more tired I felt.

"Let's go," said Petrus, getting up and offering me the cup of tea. "Drink a bit of tea, because the lady wants us to get going."

I hesitated, but I took the cup, and the hot tea revived me. I wanted to say something, ask what the animal's name was, but I could not get my voice to work. Something inside me had been aroused, something that Petrus had not taught me but that nevertheless began to manifest itself. I felt an uncontrollable desire to say strange words, the meaning of which I didn't even know. I thought that Petrus had put something in the tea. Everything began to blur, and I heard only very faintly the woman repeat to Petrus that we had to leave. I was in a state of euphoria, and I decided to speak the strange words that were coming to my mind.

All I could see in the room was the dog. When I began to say those strange words, the dog started to growl. He understood what I was saying. I became more excited and continued to speak, louder and louder. The dog rose and bared his teeth. He was no longer the docile animal I had seen on arrival but something awful and threatening that could attack me at any moment. I knew that the words were protecting me, and I began to speak even louder, focusing all of my energies on the dog. I felt that I had a different power within me and that it could keep the animal from attacking me.

From that point on, everything began to happen in slow motion. I saw the woman come toward me, shrieking and trying to push me out of the house. And I saw Petrus holding the woman back. The dog paid no attention at all to their struggle. Snarling and baring his teeth, he continued to stare at me. I was trying to understand the strange language I was speaking, but each time I stopped to think about it, my power would weaken and the dog would start coming toward me; he was growing stronger. I began to scream, giving up my attempt at understanding, and the woman began to scream, too. The dog barked and threatened me, but so long as I continued speaking, I was safe. I heard raucous laughter, but I did not know if it was really occurring or if it was in my imagination.

Suddenly, a strong wind swept through the house, and the dog howled and leapt on me. I raised my arm to protect my face, shouted something, and waited to see what the impact would be.

The dog had thrown himself upon me with all his strength, and I fell to the couch. For a few moments, our eyes were locked on each other's; in the next second, he ran from the house.

I began to cry hysterically. I thought of my family, my wife, and my friends. I experienced an enormous feeling of love and, at the same time, an absurd happiness, because all of a sudden I understood everything about the dog.

Petrus took me by the arm and led me outside, as the woman pushed us both from behind. I looked around, and there was no sign of the dog. I hugged Petrus and continued to cry as we walked along in the sunlight.

The next part of the journey is a blank; I only came to my senses later at a fountain, where Petrus was throwing water in my face and on the back of my neck. I asked for some to drink, and he said that if I drank anything then, I would vomit. I was a little nauseated, but I felt good. An immense love for everything and everybody had invaded my being. I looked around me and sensed the trees along the edge of the Road, the small fountain where we had stopped, the fresh breeze, and the bird song from the forest. I was seeing the face of my angel, as Petrus had told me I would. I asked how far we were from the woman's house, and he said we had been walking for about fifteen minutes.

"You probably want to know what happened," he said.

Actually that was not important to me at all. I was just happy about the feelings of love that permeated me. The dog, the woman, the owner of the bar, everything was a distant memory that seemed to have nothing to do with what I was feeling now. I told Petrus that I would like to go on walking because I was feeling so well.

I got up, and we returned to the Road to Santiago. Throughout the rest of the afternoon, I said almost nothing, delighting in the agreeable feeling that seemed to fill me. I still thought that perhaps Petrus had put something in the tea, but this was no longer important.

We arrived at a hotel at eight o'clock that night, and I was still in this state of beatitude, although it had diminished somewhat. The owner asked me for my passport so that I could register, and I gave it to him.

"You're from Brazil? I've been there. I stayed at a hotel on Ipanema Beach."

That absurd message brought me back to reality. There, along the Jacobean route, in a town that had been built centuries ago was a hotel keeper who had been to Ipanema Beach.

"I'm ready to talk," I told Petrus. "I have to know what happened today."

The sense of beatitude had passed. Reason took its place, and my fear of the unknown, along with an urgent need to get my feet back on the ground, had returned.

"After we eat," said Petrus.

Petrus asked the hotel owner to turn on the television but to leave the sound off. He said that this was the best way for me to hear everything he said without asking a lot of questions, because part of me would be watching the television screen. He asked me how much I remembered of what had happened. I answered that I remembered everything except the part where we had walked to the fountain.

"That part is not important to the story," he answered. On the television screen, a film having something to do with coal mines began. The actors were dressed in turn-of-the-century clothing.

"Yesterday, when I sensed the urgency in your messenger, I knew that a battle along the Road to Santiago was about to begin. You are here to find your sword and learn the RAM practices. But every time a guide leads a pilgrim, there is at least one situation that goes beyond the control of both of them. It represents a kind of practical test of what is being taught. In your case, this was the encounter with the dog.

"The details of the battle and the explanation for the many devils that can be present in an animal I will explain later. What is important now is that you understand that the woman was already used to the curse. She had accepted it as normal, and the attitudes of the world were fine with her. She had learned to be satisfied with very little.

"When you exorcised the poor old woman's demons, you also unbalanced her universe. The other day we talked about the cruelty that people are capable of inflicting on themselves. Often, when we try to demonstrate that life is good and generous, such people reject the idea as if it came from the devil. People don't like to ask too much of life because they are afraid they will be defeated. But if someone wants to fight the good fight, that person must view the world as if it were a marvelous treasure waiting to be discovered and won."

Petrus asked me if I knew what I was doing there on the Road to Santiago.

"I am searching for my sword," I answered.

"And what do you want your sword for?"

"I want it because it will bring me the power and the wisdom of the Tradition."

I felt that he was not too happy with my response. But he continued, "You are here, searching for a reward. You are daring to dream, and you are doing everything possible to make your dream come true. You need to have a better idea of what it is that you are going to do with your sword; this has to be clearer to you before we can find it. But there is one thing in your favor: you are looking for a reward. You are walking the Road to Santiago only because you want to be rewarded for your effort. I have noticed that you have applied everything I have taught you; you have been looking for a practical outcome. That is very positive.

"The only thing missing is your learning how to combine the RAM practices with your own intuition. The language of your heart is what is going to determine the best way to find and use your sword. If you can't bring the two together, the exercises and the RAM practices will become simply a part of the useless wisdom of the Tradition."

Petrus had told me this before, in a different way, and although I agreed with him, it wasn't what I wanted to hear about. There were two aspects of the experience that I could not understand: the strange language I had spoken and my feeling of love and happiness after having evicted the dog.

"The sensation of happiness occurred because your action was suffused with agape."

"You talk a lot about agape, but you haven't really explained to me what it is. I have a feeling we are dealing with something that relates to a higher form of love."

"That's exactly right. In a little while, the time will come for you to experience that intense love—the love that consumes the one who loves. Meanwhile, be happy knowing that this love has manifested itself freely in you."

"I have had this sensation before, but it was brief, and it was different somehow. It always happened after a professional triumph, a win, or when I felt that Lady Luck was being generous with me. But when the feeling arose, I always pulled back; I felt frightened of experiencing it too intensely—as if the happiness could cause envy in others or as if I were unworthy of it."

"All of us, before we learn about agape, act that way," he said, with his gaze on the television screen.

I asked him about the strange language I had spoken.

"That was a surprise to me. That is not a practice of the Road to Santiago. It is a divine grace, and it is one of the RAM practices for the Road to Rome."

I had already heard some things about the divine graces, but I asked Petrus to explain them to me.

"They are gifts from the Holy Ghost that manifest themselves in people. There are a number of different kinds: the gift of curing, the gift of miracles, the gift of prophecy, among others. You experienced the gift of tongues, which is what the apostles experienced at Pentecost.

"The gift of tongues is related to direct communication with the Holy Ghost. It is used in powerful oratory, in exorcisms—as was your case—and in wisdom. Your days on the Road and the RAM practices not only led to the danger that the dog represented for you but also by chance gave rise to the gift of tongues. It won't happen again, unless you find your sword and decide to walk the Road to Rome. In any case, it was a good omen."

I watched the silent television screen. The story of the coal mines had been transformed into a succession of men and women talking and arguing. Every so often, an actor and an actress would kiss.

"One other thing," said Petrus. "It may be that you are going to meet up with that dog again. Next time, don't try to invoke the gift of tongues, because it won't come back. Trust in what your intuition is going to tell you. I am going to teach you another RAM practice that will enhance your intuition. With it, you will begin to learn the secret language of your mind, and that language will be very useful to you for the rest of your life."

Petrus turned the television off, just as I was beginning to get involved in the story. He went to the bar and asked for a bottle of mineral water. We each drank a little, and he took what was left outdoors.

We felt the fresh air, and for a few moments neither of us said anything. The night was quiet, and the Milky Way overhead reminded me again that my goal was to find my sword.

After some time, Petrus taught me the Water Exercise.

"I'm tired; I'm going to bed," he said. "But do this exercise now. Call up your intuition again, your secret side. Don't be concerned about logic, because water is a fluid element, and it does not allow itself to be controlled easily. But water, little by little and in a nonviolent way, is going to build a new relationship between you and your universe."

And before he went through the door of the hotel, he added, "It is not often that someone gets help from a dog."

I continued to enjoy the freshness and the silence of the night. The hotel was out in the country, and there was no one there with me. I remembered the owner, who had been to

THE AROUSAL OF INTUITION
(The Water Exercise)

Make a puddle of water on a smooth, nonabsorbent surface. Look into the puddle for a while. Then, begin to play with it, without any particular commitment or objective. Make designs that mean absolutely nothing.

Do this exercise for a week, allowing at least ten minutes each time.

Don't look for practical results from this exercise; it is simply calling up your intuition, little by little. When this intuition begins to manifest itself at other times of the day, always trust in it.

Ipanema; he must find it absurd to see me there in that arid place, burned by the sun that shone down with such ferocity day after day.

I was getting sleepy, so I decided to do the exercise right away. I emptied the remaining water onto the cement and a small puddle formed. I did not have any image or shape in mind, and I wasn't seeking one. I swirled my fingers through the cold water, and I experienced the same kind of hypnosis that one feels when staring into the flames of a fire. I thought about nothing; I was just playing—playing with a puddle of water. I made some streaks at the edge of the puddle, and it seemed to become a wet sun; but the streaks quickly rejoined the puddle and disappeared. With the palm of my hand, I batted at the center of the puddle; the water splashed away, covering the cement with droplets, black stars on a gray background. I was completely lost in that absurd exercise, an exercise that had not the slightest purpose but was delightful to do. I felt that my mind had stopped working almost completely, a feeling I had previously achieved only after long periods of meditation and relaxation. At the same time, something told me that down deep, in places that my mind could not reach, a force was being born and becoming ready to manifest itself.

I stayed there for quite a while playing with the puddle, and it was difficult to give up the exercise. If Petrus had taught me the water exercise at the beginning of the journey, there is no doubt that I would have found it to be a waste of time. But now, having spoken in strange tongues and having exorcised devils, that puddle of water established a contact—however fragile—with the Milky Way above me. It reflected the stars, created designs I could not understand, and gave me the feeling not that I was wasting time but that I was creating a new code for communicating with the world.

It was the soul's secret code—the language that we know but so seldom hear.

When I came back to myself, it was late. The lights at the door had been turned off, and I entered the hotel quietly. In my room, once again I invoked Astrain. He appeared more clearly, and I spoke to him for a while about my sword and about my goals in life. For now, he made no answer, but Petrus had told me that as the invocations continued, Astrain would become a live and powerful presence at my side.

Marriage

Logroño is one of the largest cities through which pilgrims traveling the Jacobean route pass. The only other city of any size that we had entered had been Pamplona—but we had not spent the night there. On the afternoon that we arrived in Logroño, though, the city was preparing for a great festival, and Petrus suggested that we stay there, at least for one night.

I was used to the silence and freedom of the countryside, so the idea did not much appeal to me. It had been five days since the incident with the dog, and every night since then, I had invoked Astrain and performed the Water Exercise. I was feeling very calm, and I was more and more aware of the importance of the Road to Santiago in my life and of the question of what I was going to do after the pilgrimage had ended. The area we walked through was like a desert, the meals were seldom very good, and the long days on the Road were exhausting, but I was living my dream.

All of these feelings disappeared the day we arrived at Logroño. Instead of the warm, pure air of the fields, we found a city crowded with cars, journalists, and television equipment. Petrus went into the first bar we saw to ask what was happening.

"You didn't know? Today is the wedding of Colonel M.'s daughter," said the bartender. "We are going to have a huge public banquet in the square, and I am closing early today."

It was impossible to find rooms at a hotel, but eventually we were given lodging at the home of an elderly couple who had noticed the shells on Petrus's knapsack. We showered, I put on the only trousers that I had brought, and we left for the town square.

Dozens of workers, perspiring in their black suits, were putting the finishing touches on the tables that had been placed all over the square. National television crews were filming the preparations. We went down a narrow street that led to the church of the Royal Santiago parish, where the ceremony was about to begin.

Flocking to the church were great numbers of well-dressed people. The women's makeup was running in the heat, and their children, dressed in white, were irritable. Some fireworks were exploding overhead as a long black limousine stopped at the main gate. It was the groom arriving. There was no room for Petrus and me in the church, so we decided to go back to the square.

Petrus wanted to scout around, but I sat down on one of the benches, waiting for the ceremony to end and the banquet to begin. Nearby, a popcorn vendor, hoping for a windfall profit, awaited the crowd from the church.

"Are you one of the invited guests?" he asked me.

"No," I answered. "We are pilgrims on our way to Compostela."

"There's a train that goes there straight from Madrid, and if you leave on a Friday, you get your hotel free."

"Yes, but we are doing a pilgrimage."

The vendor looked at me and said respectfully, "Pilgrimages are made by saints."

I decided not to get into that discussion. He said that his daughter had already been married but was now separated from her husband.

"In Franco's time, there was more respect," he said. "Nowadays, no one cares about the family."

Despite my being in a strange country, where it is never advisable to talk politics, I could not let this pass without a response. I said that Franco had been a dictator and that nothing during his time could have been better than now.

The vendor's face turned red.

"Who do you think you are, talking like that?"

"I know this country's history. I know the war the people fought for their freedom. I have read about the crimes of the Franco forces during the Spanish civil war."

"Well, I fought in that war. I was there when my family's blood was spilled. Whatever stories you have read don't interest me; what I'm concerned about is what happens to my family. I fought against Franco, but when he won the war, life was better for me. I'm not a beggar, and I have my little popcorn stand. It wasn't this socialist government we have now that helped me. I'm worse off now than I was before."

I remembered what Petrus had said about people being content with very little. I decided not to press my point of view, and I moved to another bench.

When Petrus came back, I told him about my exchange with the popcorn vendor.

"Conversation is useful," he said, "when people want to convince themselves that what they are saying is right. I am a member of the Italian Communist Party. But I didn't know about this fascist side of you."

"What do you mean, fascist side?" I asked him angrily.

"Well, you helped the popcorn man to convince himself that Franco was good. Maybe he never knew why. Now he knows."

"Well, I'm just as surprised to learn that the ICP believes in the gifts of the Holy Ghost."

"Well, I have to be careful about what the neighbors will think," he said, laughing.

The fireworks started up again, as musicians climbed to the bandstand and tuned their instruments. The festival was about to begin.

I looked up at the sky. It was growing dark, and the stars were beginning to appear. Petrus went over to one of the waiters and brought back two plastic cups full of wine.

"It is good luck to have a drink before the party begins," he said, handing me one of the cups. "Have some of this. It will help you forget about the popcorn man."

"I wasn't even thinking about him anymore."

"Well, you should. Because what happened with him is an example of mistaken behavior. We are always trying to convert people to a belief in our own explanation of the universe. We think that the more people there are who believe as we do, the more certain it will be that what we believe is the truth. But it doesn't work that way at all.

"Look around. Here is a huge party about to begin. A commemoration. Many different things are being celebrated simultaneously: the father's hope that his daughter would marry, the daughter's wish for the same thing, the groom's dreams. That's good, because they believe in their dreams and want to demonstrate to everyone that they have achieved their goals. It is not a party that is being held to convince anyone of anything, so it's going to be a lot of fun. From what I can see, they are people who have fought the good fight of love."

"But you are trying to convince me, Petrus, by guiding me along the Road to Santiago."

He gave me a cold look.

"I am only teaching you the RAM practices. But you will find your sword only if you discover that the Road and the truth and the life are in your heart."

Petrus pointed to the sky, where the stars were now clearly visible.

"There is no religion that is capable of bringing all of the stars together, because if this were to happen, the universe would become a gigantic, empty space and would lose its reason for existence. Every star—and every person—has their own space and their own special characteristics. There are green stars, yellow stars, blue stars, and white stars, and there are comets, meteors and meteorites, nebulas and rings. What appear from down here to be a huge number of bodies that are similar to each other are really a million different things, spread over a space that is beyond human comprehension."

A rocket from the fireworks burst, and its light obscured the sky for a moment. A shower of brilliant green streamers fell to the ground.

"Earlier, we only heard their noise because of the daylight. Now we can see their light," Petrus said. "That's the only change people can aspire to."

The bride came out of the church, and people shouted and threw their handfuls of rice. She was a thin girl of about sixteen, and she held the arm of a boy in a tuxedo. The congregation appeared and began to move toward the square.

"Look, there's the colonel. . . . Oh, look at the bride's dress. How beautiful," said some boys near us. The guests took their places at the tables, the waiters served the wine, and the band began to play. The popcorn vendor was surrounded by a mob of screaming boys who made their purchases and then scattered the empty bags on the ground. I imagined that for the townspeople of Logroño, at least that night, the rest of the world—with its threat of nuclear war, unemployment, and murders—did not exist. It was a festival night, the tables had been placed in the square for the people, and everyone felt important.

A television crew came toward us, and Petrus averted his face. But the men passed us by, heading for one of the guests who sat near us. I recognized immediately who he was: Antonio, the man who had led the Spanish fans in their cheers at the World Cup in Mexico in 1986. When the interview was over, I went up to him and told him that I was a Brazilian; feigning anger, he complained about a goal of which Spain had been robbed in the opening round of the Cup.[1]

But then he gave me a hug, and said that Brazil would soon once again have the best players in the world.

"How do you manage to see the game when your back is always to the field and you are inciting the fans," I asked. It was something I had noticed over and over again during the television transmissions of the World Cup games.

"That's what gives me satisfaction. Helping the fans believe in victory."

And then, as if he too were a guide on the Road to Santiago, he said, "Fans who lack the faith can make a team lose a game it is already winning."

Manolo was then grabbed by others who wanted to interview him, but I stood there thinking about what he had

---

[1]In the game between Spain and Brazil at that World Cup in Mexico, a Spanish goal was nullified because the referee had not seen the ball hit behind the goal line before ricocheting out. Brazil wound up winning that game 1–0.

said. Even without ever having walked the Road to Santiago, he knew what it was to fight the good fight.

I found Petrus hiding behind some trees, obviously uncomfortable with the presence of the television cameras. It was only after their lights had been turned off that he emerged from the trees and relaxed a bit. We asked for two more cups of wine, I fixed myself a plate of canapés, and Petrus found a table where we could sit with some of the guests.

The newlyweds cut into a huge wedding cake. People cheered.

"They must really love each other," I said.

"Of course they do," said a dark-suited man sitting with us. "Have you ever heard of anyone marrying for any other reason?"

I kept my answer to myself, remembering what Petrus had said about the popcorn vendor. But my guide didn't let it pass.

"Which kind of love are you talking about: eros, philos, or agape?"

The man looked at him blankly. Petrus got up, filled his cup, and asked me to walk with him.

"There are three Greek words that mean love," he began. "Today, you are seeing a manifestation of eros, the feeling of love that exists between two people."

The bride and groom were smiling for the photographers and accepting congratulations.

"It appears that these two really do love each other," he said, looking at the couple. "And they believe that their love will grow. But shortly, they will be alone with each other, struggling to earn a living, build a house, and share their adventure. This is what ennobles love and dignifies it. He will do his time in the army. She is probably a good cook and will be an excellent housewife, because she has been trained since she was a child for that role. She will be good company for him, they'll have children, and they will feel that they are building something together. They'll be fighting the good fight. So even if they have problems, they will never be really unhappy.

"However, this story that I am telling you could go a very different way. He might begin to feel that he's not free enough to express all of the eros, all of the love that he has for other women. She might begin to feel that she gave up a brilliant career in order to be with her husband. So instead of creating something together, each could begin to feel robbed of a means of expressing love. Eros, the spirit that unites them, would begin to reveal only its negative side. And what God had provided to humans as their noblest sentiment would become a source of hatred and destructiveness."

I looked around me. Eros was present in many of the relationships there. The Water Exercise had awakened the language of my heart, and I was seeing people in a different way. Maybe it was the days of solitude on the road, or maybe it was the RAM practices, but I could feel the presence of good eros and evil eros, just as Petrus had described.

"It's strange," Petrus said, sensing the same thing. "Whether it's good or evil, the face of eros is never the same for any two people. Just like the stars I was talking about half an hour ago. And no one can escape eros. Everyone needs its presence, despite the fact that many times, eros makes us feel apart from the world, trapped in our solitude."

The band began to play a waltz. The guests went to a small cement section in front of the bandstand and started to dance. The alcohol was making itself felt, and people were perspiring more and smiling more. I noticed a girl dressed in blue who looked as if she had waited for this wedding just to have the chance to dance the waltz—she wanted to dance with someone who would embrace her in the way she had dreamed of since adolescence. She was watching a well-dressed boy, who wore a white suit and stood among his friends. They were all talking and had not noticed that the waltz had begun. Nor did they see that a few yards away, a girl in a blue dress looked longingly at one of them.

I thought about small towns and marriage to the boy one has dreamed of since childhood.

The girl in blue saw that I was watching her and tried to conceal herself among her girlfriends. As she did, the boy searched for her with his eyes. When he saw that she was there with her friends, he went back to his conversation with his own group.

I pointed out the two of them to Petrus. He watched the game of glances for a while and then went back to his cup of wine.

"They act as if it were shameful to make any show of love," was all he said.

A girl near us was staring at Petrus and me. She must have been half our age. Petrus held up his cup of wine and made a toast in her direction. The girl laughed in embarrassment and pointed toward her parents, as if to explain why she did not come closer.

"That's the beautiful side of love," Petrus said. "The love that dares, the love for two older strangers who have come from nowhere and will be gone tomorrow—gone into a world where she would like to travel, too."

I could hear in his voice that the wine was having an effect on him.

"Today, we will talk of love!" said my guide, a bit loudly. "Let us speak of true love, which grows and grows, and makes the world go round, and makes people wise!"

A well-dressed woman near us seemed not to be paying any attention at all to the party. She went from table to table, straightening the cups, the china, and the silverware.

"See that woman there?" asked Petrus. "The one who's straightening things up? Well, as I said, eros has many faces, and that's another of them. That's frustrated love, with its own kind of unhappiness. She is going to kiss the bride and groom, but inside she'll be saying that a knot has been tied around them. She's trying to neaten up the world because she herself is in complete disorder. And there"—he pointed toward another couple, the wife wearing excessive makeup and an elaborate coiffure—"is eros accepted. Social love, without a vestige of passion. She has accepted her role and has severed any connection with the world or with the good fight."

"You're being very bitter, Petrus. Isn't there anyone here who can be saved?"

"Of course there is. The girl who was watching us, the adolescents that are dancing—they know only about good eros. If they don't allow themselves to be influenced by the hypocrisy of the love that dominated the past generation, the world will certainly be a different place."

He pointed to an elderly couple sitting at one of the tables.

"And those two, also. They haven't let themselves be infected by hypocrisy like the others. They look like working people. Hunger and need have required them to work together. They learned the practices you are learning without ever having heard of RAM. They find the power of love in the work they do. It's there that eros shows its most beautiful face, because it's united with that of philos."

"What is philos?"

"Philos is love in the form of friendship. It's what I feel toward you and others. When the flame of eros stops burning, it is philos that keeps a couple together."

"And agape?"

"Today's not the day to talk about agape. Agape is in both eros and philos—but that's just a phrase. Let's enjoy the rest of the party without talking about the love that consumes." And Petrus poured some more wine into his plastic cup.

The happiness around us was contagious. Petrus was getting drunk, and at first I was a little surprised. But I remembered what he had said one afternoon: that the RAM practices made sense only if they could be performed by the common people.

That night, Petrus seemed to be a person like any other. He was companionable and friendly, patting people on the back and talking to anyone who paid him any attention. A little later, he was so drunk that I had to help him back to the hotel.

On the way, I took stock of my situation. Here I was, guiding my guide. I realized that at no time during the entire journey had Petrus made any effort to appear wiser, holier, or in any way better than I. All he had done was to transmit to me his experience with the RAM practices. Beyond that, he had made a point of showing that he was just like anyone else—that he experienced eros, philos, and agape.

This realization made me feel stronger. Petrus was just another pilgrim on the Road to Santiago.

Enthusiasm

Though I speak with the tongues of men and of angels . . . and though I have the gift of prophecy . . . and have all faith so that I could remove mountains . . . and have not love, I am nothing."

Petrus was once again quoting from Saint Paul. My guide felt that the apostle Paul was the major occult interpreter of Christ's message. We were fishing that afternoon after having walked for the whole morning. No fish had yet perished on the hook, but Petrus didn't care about that at all. According to him, fishing was basically a symbol of the human being's relationship with the world: we know why we are fishing, and we will catch something if we stay with it, but whether we do or not depends on God's help.

"It's a good idea always to do something relaxing prior to making an important decision in your life," he said. "The Zen monks listen to the rocks growing. I prefer fishing."

But at that time of day, because of the heat, even the fat, lazy fish on the bottom ignored the hook. Whether the bait was up or down, the result was the same. I decided to give it up and take a walk through the nearby woods. I went as far as an old, abandoned cemetery close to the river—it had a gate that was totally disproportionate to the size of the burial ground—and then came back to where Petrus was fishing. I asked about the cemetery.

"The gate was part of an ancient hospital for pilgrims," he said. "But the hospital was abandoned, and later, someone had the idea of using the facade and building the cemetery."

"Which has also been abandoned."

"That's right. The things of this life don't last very long."

I said that he had been nasty the night before in his judgments of the people at the party, and he was surprised at me. He said that what we had talked about was no more or less than we had ourselves experienced in our personal lives. All of us seek eros, and then when eros wants to turn itself into philos, we think that love is worthless. We don't see that it is philos that leads us to the highest form of love, agape.

"Tell me more about agape," I said.

Petrus answered that agape cannot really be discussed; it has to be lived. That afternoon, if possible, he wanted to show me one of the faces of agape. But in order for this to happen, the universe, as in the business of fishing, would have to collaborate so that everything went well.

"The messenger helps you, but there is one thing that is beyond the messenger's control, beyond his desires, and beyond you, as well."

"What is that?"

"The divine spark. What we call luck."

When the sun had begun to set, we resumed our walking. The Jacobean route passed through some vineyards and fields that were completely deserted at that time of day. We crossed the main road—also deserted—and started again through the woods. In the distance, I could see the Saint Lorenzo peak, the highest point in the kingdom of Castile. I had changed a great deal since I had met Petrus for the first time near Saint-Jean-Pied-de-Port. Brazil and the business deals that I had been worried about had practically vanished from my mind. The only important thing for me now was my objective. I discussed it every night with Astrain, who was becoming clearer and clearer for me. I was able to see him, seated at my side, any time I tried. I learned that he had a nervous tic in his right eye and that he had the habit of smiling disdainfully every time I repeated something as evidence that I had understood what he was saying. A few weeks earlier—during the first days of the pilgrimage—I had been afraid that I would never complete it. When we had passed through Roncesvalles, I had been very disillusioned about everything to do with the journey. I had wanted to get to Santiago immediately, recover my sword, and get back to fighting what Petrus called the good fight.[1] But right now, with my connection to civilization severed, what was most important was the sun on my head and the possibility that I might experience agape.

We went down the bank of an arroyo, crossed the dry bed, and had to struggle to climb up the other side. An impressive river must have flowed there once, washing away the bottom in its search for the depths and secrets of the earth. Now the riverbed was so dry that it could be crossed on foot. But the river's major accomplishment, the valley it had created, was still there, and it took a major effort to climb out of it. "Nothing in this life endures," Petrus had said a few hours before.

"Petrus, have you ever been in love?"

The question was a spontaneous one, and I was surprised at my courage. Up until then, I had known only the bare outline of my guide's private life.

---

[1] I found out later that the term had actually been created by Saint Paul.

"I have known a lot of women, if that is what you mean. And I have really loved each of them. But I experienced agape only with two."

I told him that I had been in love many times but had been worried about whether I could ever become serious with anyone. If I had continued that way, it would have led to a solitary old age, and I had been very fearful of this.

"I don't think you look to love as a means to a comfortable retirement."

It was almost nine o'clock before it began to get dark. The vineyards were behind us, and we were walking through an arid landscape. I looked around and could see in the distance a small hermitage in the rocks, similar to many others we had passed on our pilgrimage. We walked on for a while, and then, detouring from the yellow markers, we approached the small building.

When we were close enough, Petrus called out a name that I didn't understand, and he stopped to listen for an answer. We heard nothing. Petrus called again, but no one answered.

"Let's go, anyway," he said. And we moved forward.

The hermitage consisted of just four whitewashed walls. The door was open—or rather, there really was no door, just a small entry panel, half a meter high, which hung precariously by one hinge. Within, there was a stone fireplace and some basins stacked on the floor. Two of them were filled with wheat and potatoes.

We sat down in the silence. Petrus lit a cigarette and said we should wait. My legs were hurting, but something in that hermitage, rather than calming me, made me feel excited. It would also have frightened me a little if Petrus had not been there.

"Where does whoever lives here sleep?" I asked, just to break the uneasy silence.

"There, where you are sitting," Petrus said, pointing to the bare earth. I said something about moving to another spot, but he told me to stay exactly where I was. The temperature must have been dropping, because I began to feel cold.

We waited for almost an hour. Petrus called out the strange name several more times and then gave up. Just when I expected us to get up and leave, he began to speak.

"Present here is one of the two manifestations of agape," he said, as he stubbed out his third cigarette. "It is not the only one, but it is the purest. Agape is total love. It is the love that consumes the person who experiences it. Whoever knows and experiences agape learns that nothing else in the world is important—just love. This was the kind of love that Jesus felt for humanity, and it was so great that it shook the stars and changed the course of history. His solitary life enabled him to accomplish things that kings, armies, and empires could not.

"During the millennia of Christian civilization, many individuals have been seized by this love that consumes. They had so much to give—and their world demanded so little—that they went out into the deserts and to isolated places, because the love they felt was so great that it transformed them. They became the hermit saints that we know today.

"For you and for me, who experience a different form of agape, this life may seem terrible. But the love that consumes makes everything else—absolutely everything—lose its importance. Those men lived just to be consumed by their love."

Petrus told me that a monk named Alfonso lived there. Petrus had met him on his first pilgrimage to Compostela, as he was picking fruit to eat. His guide, a much more enlightened man than he, was a friend of Alfonso's, and the three of them had together performed the Ritual of Agape, the Blue Sphere Exercise. Petrus said that it had been one of the most important experiences of his life and that even today when he performed the exercise, he remembered the hermitage and Alfonso. There was more emotion in his voice than I had ever heard from him.

"Agape is the love that consumes," he repeated, as if that were the phrase that best defined this strange kind of love. "Martin Luther King once said that when Christ spoke of loving one's enemies, he was referring to agape. Because according to him, it was 'impossible to like our enemies, those who were cruel to us, those who tried to make our day-to-day suffering even worse.' But agape is much more than liking. It is a feeling that suffuses, that fills every space in us, and turns our aggression to dust.

"You have learned how to be reborn, how to stop being cruel to yourself, and how to communicate with your messenger. But everything you do from now on and every good result that you take with you from the Road to Santiago will make sense only you have also experienced the love that consumes."

I reminded Petrus that he had said that there were two forms of agape. And that he probably had not experienced this first form, since he had not become a hermit.

"You're right. You and I and most pilgrims who walk the Road to Santiago, learning the RAM practices, experience agape in its other form: enthusiasm.

"For the ancients, enthusiasm meant trance, or ecstasy— a connection with God. Enthusiasm is agape directed at a particular idea or a specific thing. We have all experienced it. When we love and believe from the bottom of our heart, we feel ourselves to be stronger than anyone in the world, and we feel a serenity that is based on the certainty that nothing can shake our faith. This unusual strength allows us always to make the right decision at the right time, and when we achieve our goal, we are amazed at our own capabilities. Because when we are involved in the good fight, nothing else is important; enthusiasm carries us toward our goal.

"Enthusiasm normally manifests itself with all of its force during the first years of our lives. At that time, we still have strong links with the divinity, and we throw ourselves into our play with our toys with such a will that dolls take on life and our tin soldiers actually march. When Jesus said that the kingdom of heaven belonged to the children, he was referring to agape in the form of enthusiasm. Children were attracted to him, not because they understood his miracles, his wisdom, or his Pharisees and apostles. They went to him in joy, moved by enthusiasm."

I told Petrus that on that very afternoon, I had realized that I was completely absorbed by the Road to Santiago. Those days and nights in Spain had almost made me forget about my sword, and they were a unique experience. Most other things had lost their importance.

"This afternoon, we were trying to fish, but the fish would not bite," said Petrus. "Normally, we allow enthusiasm to elude us when we are involved in such mundane activities, those that have no importance at all in the overall scale of our existence. We lose our enthusiasm because of the small and unavoidable defeats we suffer during the good fight. And since we don't realize that enthusiasm is a major strength, able to help us win the ultimate victory, we let it dribble through our fingers; we do this without recognizing that we are letting the true meaning of our lives escape us. We blame the world for our boredom and for our losses, and we forget that it was we ourselves who allowed this enchanting power, which justifies everything, to diminish—the manifestation of agape in the form of enthusiasm."

I remembered the cemetery near the river. That strange, unusually large portal was a perfect representation of what had been lost. And beyond it, only the dead.

As if he had guessed what I was thinking, Petrus began to talk about something that was similar.

"A few days ago, you must have been surprised when I got so angry with that poor waiter who had spilled coffee on my shorts—shorts that were already filthy with the dust and dirt of the road. Actually, I was nervous because I saw in the boy's eyes that his enthusiasm was draining away like the blood that runs from wrists that have been slashed. I saw that boy, so strong and full of life, beginning to die because inside him, moment by moment, agape was perishing. I have been around for a long time, and I have learned to live with these things, but that lad, with the way he behaved and with all the good things I felt that he could bring to humanity, left me shocked and sad. But I know that my anger wounded him a bit and stemmed the death of agape.

"In the same vein, when you exorcised that woman's dog, you felt agape in its purest form. It was a noble deed, and it made me proud to be here serving as your guide. So for the first time in our experience on the Road, I am going to participate in an exercise with you."

And Petrus taught me the Ritual of Agape, the Blue Sphere Exercise.

"I am going to help you to arouse your enthusiasm, to create a power that is going to expand like a blue sphere that encloses the entire planet," he said, "to show that I respect you and what you are doing."

Up until then, Petrus had never expressed an opinion, either favorable or unfavorable, regarding the way in which I performed the exercises. He had helped me to interpret my first contact with the messenger, and he had rescued me from the trance of the Seed Exercise, but he had never expressed any interest in the results I had achieved. More than once I had asked him why he did not want to know about my feelings, and he had answered that his only obligation as my guide was to show me the Road and to teach me the RAM practices. It was up to me whether I enjoyed the results or found them to be unpleasant.

When he said that he was going to participate with me in the exercise, I suddenly felt unworthy of his praise. I knew my faults, and many times I had doubted whether he could succeed in guiding me along the Road. I wanted to say all this to him, but he interrupted me before I could begin.

"Don't be cruel with yourself, or you will not have learned the lesson I taught you before. Be kind. Accept the praise that you deserve."

Tears came to my eyes. Petrus led me outside. The night was darker than usual. I sat down next to him, and we began to sing. The melody came from within me, and he accompanied me with no effort. I began to clap my hands softly, as I rocked forward and back. My clapping increased in its intensity, and the music flowed from me, a psalm of praise to the darkness of the sky, the deserted plateau, and the lifeless stones around us. I began to see the saints that I had believed in as a child, and I could sense that life had gotten away from me because of my having killed a great deal of my agape. But now the love that consumes returned, and the saints smiled from the heavens with the same look and intensity that I had seen in them when I was small.

I spread my arms so that agape could flow, and a mysterious current of bright blue light began to wash through me, cleansing my soul and pardoning my sins. The light spread first to our surroundings and then enveloped the world, and I started to weep. I wept because I was reexperiencing the enthusiasm of my childhood; I was once again a child, and nothing in the world could cause me harm. I felt a presence

THE BLUE SPHERE EXERCISE

Seat yourself comfortably, and relax. Try not to think about anything.

1. Feel how good it is to be alive. Let your heart feel free and affectionate; let it rise above and beyond the details of the problems that may be bothering you. Begin to sing softly a song from your childhood. Imagine that your heart is growing, filling the room—and later your home—with an intense, shining blue light.

2. When you reach this point, begin to sense the presence of the saints (or other beings) in which you placed your faith when you were a child. Notice that they are present, arriving from everywhere, smiling and giving you faith and confidence.

3. Picture the saints approaching you, placing their hands on your head and wishing you love, peace, and communion with the world—the communion of the saints.

4. When this sensation becomes strong, feel that the blue light is a current that enters you and leaves you like a shining, flowing river. This blue light begins to spread through your house, then through your neighborhood, your city, and your country; it eventually envelops the world in an immense blue sphere. This is the manifestation of the great love that goes beyond the day-to-day struggle; it reinforces and invigorates, as it provides energy and peace.

5. Keep the light spread around the world for as long as possible. Your heart is open, spreading love. This phase of the exercise should last for a minimum of five minutes.

6. Come out of your trance, bit by bit, and return to reality. The saints will remain near. The blue light will continue to spread around the world.

This ritual can and should be done with more than one person. When this is the case, the participants should hold hands while they do the exercise.

draw near and sit down to my right. I imagined that it was my messenger and that he was the only one who could perceive the strong blue light that was entering me and leaving me, spreading throughout the world.

The light was increasing in its intensity, and I felt that as it enclosed the world, it penetrated into every door and every back alley, touching every person alive for at least a fraction of a second.

I felt my hands being held open and extended to the heavens. At that moment, the flow of the blue light increased and became so strong that I thought I was going to pass out. But I was able to keep the light alive for a few moments more, until I reached the end of the song I was singing.

I was exhausted but relaxed; I felt free and content with life and with what I had just done. The hands that held mine released me. I saw that one of them was Petrus's, and I knew in my heart who it was that held the other.

I opened my eyes, and there at my side was the monk, Alfonso. He smiled and said, *"Buenas noches."* I smiled, too, and I seized his hand and held it tightly to my breast. He allowed me to do this for a moment and then gently removed his hand.

None of us spoke. Some time later, Alfonso arose and continued his trek along the rocky plateau. I watched him until he was completely hidden by the darkness.

Petrus broke the silence then, but he made no mention of Alfonso.

"Do this exercise whenever you can, and soon agape will live once again within you. Repeat it before you embark on any project, during the first days of any trip, or when you have been greatly affected by something. If possible, do it with someone you like. It is an exercise that should be shared."

So there was the old Petrus: coach, instructor, and guide, the man about whom I knew so little. The emotion that he had shown in the hermitage had already passed away. But when he had touched my hand during the exercise, I had felt the greatness of his soul.

We returned to the hermitage where we had left our things.

"The occupant won't be back today, so I think we can sleep here," said Petrus, lying down. I unrolled my sleeping bag, took a swallow of wine, and lay down. I was exhausted by the love that consumes. But it was a tiredness that was free of tension, and before I closed my eyes, I thought of the thin, bearded monk who had sat beside me and wished me good night. Somewhere out there he was being consumed by the divine flame. Maybe that was why the night was so unusually dark—he had taken all the light of the world into himself.

Death

Are you pilgrims?" asked the old woman who served us our breakfast. We were in Azofra, a village of small houses, each with a medieval shield embossed on its facade. We had filled our canteens at the village fountain a few moments earlier.

I said that we were, and the woman's eyes glowed with respect and pride.

"When I was a girl, at least one pilgrim passed through here every day, bound for Compostela. After the war and after Franco, I don't know what happened, but the pilgrimages stopped. Someone must have built a highway. Nowadays, people only want to travel by car."

Petrus said nothing. He had awakened in a bad mood. I nodded in agreement with the old woman and pictured a new, paved expressway, climbing the mountains and running across the valleys, automobiles with scallop shells painted on their hoods, and souvenir shops at the gates of the monasteries. I finished my coffee and bread dipped in olive oil. Looking at Aymeric Picaud's guide, I estimated that we should arrive that afternoon in Santo Domingo de la Calzada, and I was planning to sleep at the Parador Nacional.[1]

I was spending much less money than I had planned, even eating three meals a day. It was time for an extravagance, time to give my body the same treatment I had been giving my stomach.

I had awakened with a strange feeling of being in a hurry and of wanting to be in Santo Domingo already. I had experienced the same feeling two days earlier, when we had walked to the hermitage. Petrus was more melancholy and quiet than usual; was this the result of our meeting with Alfonso two days ago? I felt a strong need to invoke Astrain so that we could discuss the matter. But I had never summoned him in the morning, and I was not sure that I could. I decided against it.

We finished our coffee and began to walk. We passed a medieval house with its coat of arms, the ruins of an ancient hostel for pilgrims, and a park on the outskirts of the village. As I once again readied myself to move out across the countryside, I felt a strong presence to my left side. I walked on, but Petrus stopped me.

"There is no use running away," he said. "Stop and deal with it."

I wanted to get away from Petrus and keep going. I had a disagreeable feeling, a kind of colic near my stomach. For a few moments, I tried to believe that it was caused by the bread with olive oil, but I knew that I had felt it earlier in the day and I could not fool myself. It was tension—tension and fear.

"Look behind you." Petrus's voice had an urgency to it. "Look before it's too late!"

---

[1] The Paradores Nacionales are ancient castles and historic monuments that have been turned into first-class hotels by the Spanish government.

116

I spun around quickly. To my left was an abandoned house, its vegetation burned by the sun. An olive tree raised its twisted branches to the sky. And between the tree and the house, looking fixedly at me, was a dog.

A black dog, the same dog that I had banished from the woman's house a few days earlier.

I forgot all about Petrus and looked squarely into the dog's eyes. Something inside me—perhaps it was the voice of Astrain or of my guardian angel—told me that if I averted my eyes, the dog would attack me. We remained that way, staring at each other, for some time. Here I was, I thought, after having experienced the wonder of the love that consumes, once again about to be confronted by the daily and constant threats to my existence that the world would always present. I wondered why the animal had followed me for such a great distance and what it was that he wanted; after all, I was just a pilgrim in quest of my sword, and I had neither the desire nor the patience for problems with people or animals. I tried to say this to him with my eyes—remembering the monks at the convent who communicated through their eyes—but the dog did not move. He continued to stare at me, without emotion, but he appeared ready to attack should I become distracted or show fear.

Fear! I could sense that my fear had vanished. I thought the situation too stupid for fear. My stomach was knotted up, and I felt like vomiting, but I wasn't frightened. If I had been, something told me that my eyes would have given me away, and the animal would try to overcome me, as he had before. I did not want to avert my eyes, even when I sensed that a figure was approaching along a narrow road to my right.

The figure stopped for an instant and then came directly toward us. It crossed my line of sight as I stared at the dog, and this person said something I could not understand in a feminine voice. Its presence was good—friendly and positive.

In the fraction of a second during which the image had crossed my line of sight, my stomach relaxed. I felt that I had a powerful friend who was there to help me through this absurd, unnecessary conflict. When the figure had passed by, the dog lowered his eyes. Then he jumped, ran behind the abandoned house, and disappeared from view.

It was only then that my heart began to react. The tachycardia was so strong that I felt dizzy and faint. As the scene around me spun, I looked along the road that Petrus and I had walked only a few minutes earlier, seeking the figure that had given me the strength to defeat the dog. It was a nun. Her back was to me, and she was walking toward Azofra. I could not see her face, but I remembered her voice, and I guessed that she was in her early twenties. I looked in the direction from which she had come: she had appeared from a narrow path that seemed to lead nowhere.

"It was she . . . it was she who helped me," I murmured, as my dizziness grew worse.

"Don't start creating fantasies in a world that is already extraordinary," said Petrus, supporting me by the arm. "She comes from a convent in Cañas, three or four miles from here. You can't see it from here."

My heart was still pounding, and I was sure I was going to be sick. I was too upset to speak or ask for an explanation. I sat down on the ground, and Petrus threw some water on my forehead and on the nape of my neck. I remembered that he had done the same thing after we had left the woman's house—but that day I had cried for joy. Now the sensation was just the opposite.

Petrus let me rest a bit. The water brought me around, and the nausea began to subside. Things slowly returned to normal. When I felt restored, Petrus said we should walk a little, and I obeyed. We walked for about fifteen minutes, but the exhaustion returned. We sat down at the foot of a *rollo*, a medieval column supporting a cross. Such columns marked a number of stretches along the Jacobean route.

"Your fear has hurt you much more than the dog did," said Petrus, as I rested.

I wanted to understand that absurd encounter.

"In the life on the Road to Santiago, certain things happen that are beyond our control. When we first met, I told you that I had read in the gypsy's eyes the name of the demon you would have to confront. I was surprised to learn that the demon was a dog, but I did not say anything to you about it at the time. Only after we arrived at that woman's house—when for the first time, you showed the love that consumes—did I see your enemy.

"When you chased away that woman's dog, you did not place him anywhere. You didn't hurl the spirits into a drove of pigs that was thrown over a precipice, as Jesus did. You simply chased the dog away. Now his force wanders along behind you, without a destination. Before finding your sword, you are going to have to decide whether you want to be enslaved by that force or whether you will dominate it."

My fatigue began to pass. I took a deep breath and felt the cold stone of the *rollo* against my back. Petrus gave me some more water and went on:

"Cases of obsession occur when people lose their mastery over the forces of the earth. The gypsy's curse had frightened that woman, and her fear had opened a breach that the messenger of death was then able to penetrate. This doesn't always happen, but neither is it rare. Your confidence and your sense of mastery depend a great deal on how you react to threats made by others."

This time it was I who remembered a passage from the Bible. A verse in the Book of Job says, "For the thing that I greatly feared is come upon me."

"A threat leads to nothing if it is not accepted. In fighting the good fight, you should never forget that. Just as you should never forget that both attacking and fleeing are part of the fight. What isn't a part of the fight is becoming paralyzed by fear."

I had not felt fear when the dog was there. This had surprised me, and I told Petrus about it.

"I could see that you felt no fear. If you had, the dog would have attacked you. And without a doubt, he would have won the fight. Because the dog was not afraid either. The strangest thing, though, was the arrival of that nun. When you sensed the presence of something positive, your imagination concluded that someone had arrived to help you. And this, your faith, saved you. Even though it was based on an assumption that was absolutely false."

Petrus was right. He laughed at me, and I laughed, too. We got up to resume our walking. I was already feeling better.

"There is one thing you have to know, though," said Petrus as we moved on. "The duel with the dog will end only with a victory for you or for him. He will be back, and the next time you must try to take the fight through to the end. If you don't, his presence will worry you for the rest of your life."

In the encounter with the gypsy, Petrus had told me, he had learned the name of the demon. I asked him what it was.

"Legion," he answered. "Because he is many."

We passed through fields that the farmers were preparing for sowing. Here and there, some peasants operated crude water pumps in the centuries-old fight against the arid soil. Along the edge of the Road to Santiago, stones had been piled into endless walls, crisscrossing the fields. I thought about how, in spite of all the centuries during which that soil had been worked, stones still surfaced—stones that could break the blade of a plow, render a horse lame, and leave calluses on the peasants' hands. It was a battle every year, a battle that would never end.

Petrus was quieter than usual, and I realized that he had said almost nothing since morning. After our conversation at the medieval *rollo,* he had been mute, not answering any of the questions I had asked. I wanted to know more about the "many demons," because he had already explained to me that each person has only one messenger. But Petrus was not interested in talking about it, and I decided to wait for a better time.

We climbed a small rise, and from the top we could see the main tower of the church at Santo Domingo de la Calzada. I was glad to see it; I began to think about the magical comfort of the Parador Nacional. From what I had read about it, the building had been constructed by Santo Domingo himself as a shelter for pilgrims. Saint Francis of Assisi had stayed there on his way to Compostela. Everything about it excited me.

At about seven o'clock that evening, Petrus said we should stop. I was reminded of Roncesvalles and of the slow pace we had taken when I had needed some wine to warm me, and I was afraid that he was preparing something like that.

"A messenger would never help you to defeat someone else. Messengers are neither good nor bad, as I have already told you, but they have a sense of loyalty among themselves. Don't rely on your messenger to help you defeat the dog."

Now it was my turn not to want to talk about messengers. I wanted to get to Santo Domingo.

"The messengers of people who have died can occupy the body of someone who is dominated by fear. That is why, in the case of the dog, he is many. Messengers were invited in by the woman's fear—not just the murdered gypsy's messenger but all of the many messengers who wander in space, seeking a way to establish contact with the forces of the earth."

He was finally answering my question, but there was something in the way he spoke that seemed artificial, as if this were not what he really wanted to say. My instincts told me to be wary.

"What do you want, Petrus?" I asked him, a bit irritated.

My guide did not answer. He walked into the field toward an ancient, almost leafless tree that stood about thirty yards from us. It was the only tree visible on the entire horizon. Since he had not given me the signal to follow, I stood where I was. And I saw a strange thing happen: Petrus walked around the tree several times and said something out loud, while he looked at the ground. When he had finished, he gestured for me to come over.

"Sit here," he said. There was a different tone to his voice, and I couldn't tell whether it was friendliness or irritation. "Stay here. I will see you tomorrow in Santo Domingo de la Calzada."

Before I could say a word, Petrus continued, "One of these days—and I guarantee you that it will not be today—you are going to have to confront the most important enemy you will meet on the Road to Santiago: the dog. When that day comes, you can be sure that I will be close at hand and will give you the strength you need to fight him. But today you are going to confront a different type of enemy, an unreal enemy that may destroy you or may turn out to be your best friend: death.

"Human beings are the only ones in nature who are aware that they will die. For that reason and only for that reason, I

122

have a profound respect for the human race, and I believe that its future is going to be much better than its present. Even knowing that their days are numbered and that everything will end when they least expect it, people make of their lives a battle that is worthy of a being with eternal life. What people regard as vanity—leaving great works, having children, acting in such a way as to prevent one's name from being forgotten—I regard as the highest expression of human dignity.

"Still, being fragile creatures, humans always try to hide from themselves the certainty that they will die. They do not see that it is death itself that motivates them to do the best things in their lives. They are afraid to step into the dark, afraid of the unknown, and their only way of conquering that fear is to ignore the fact that their days are numbered. They do not see that with an awareness of death, they would be able to be even more daring, to go much further in their daily conquests, because then they would have nothing to lose—for death is inevitable."

The possibility of spending the night in Santo Domingo was looking more and more remote. But now I was interested in what Petrus was saying. The sun itself was dying beyond the horizon there in front of us.

"Death is our constant companion, and it is death that gives each person's life its true meaning. But in order to see the real face of our death, we first have to know all of the anxieties and terrors that the simple mention of its name is able to evoke in any human being."

Petrus sat down beside me under the tree. He said that he had circled its trunk a few minutes before because it reminded him of everything that had happened to him when he had been a pilgrim bound for Santiago. Then he took from his knapsack two sandwiches that he had bought at lunchtime.

"Here, where you are now, there is no danger," he said, giving me the sandwiches. "There are no poisonous snakes,

and the dog will return to attack you only after he has forgotten this morning's defeat. And there are no bandits or crim-
inals around here. You are in a spot that is absolutely safe, with
one exception: the danger created by your own fear."

Petrus pointed out to me that two days earlier, I had experienced a sensation that had been as intense and as violent as death itself—that of the love that consumes. And that
at one point I had vacillated and been afraid. He said that I
had been afraid because I knew nothing about universal love.
He explained to me that although all of us have some idea
of death, we do not see that death is only another manifestation of agape. I answered that with all of my years of train-
ing in magic, I had practically lost my fear of death. Actually,
I was more frightened by the way in which I would die than
by death itself.

"Well, then, tonight take a look at the most frightening
way to die."

And at that point, Petrus taught me the Buried Alive
Exercise.

"You should do this exercise only once," he said. I was
thinking of an exercise from the theater that was quite similar. "It is important that you be as truthful with yourself as
possible and that you be as fearful as necessary for the exercise to get at the roots of your soul; it has to strip away the
scary mask that hides the gentle face of your death."

Petrus stood up, and I saw his silhouette against the
background of the setting sun. From where I was seated, he
seemed to be a gigantic and powerful figure.

"Petrus, I have one more question."

"What is it?"

"This morning you were close-mouthed and strange.
You sensed before I did that the dog was going to appear.
How was that possible?"

124

THE BURIED ALIVE EXERCISE

Lie down on the floor and relax. Cross your arms over your chest in the posture of death.

Imagine all of the details of your burial, as if it were to be carried out tomorrow, the only difference being that you are being buried alive. As the situation develops in your mind—the chapel, the procession to the cemetery, the lowering of the casket, the worms in the grave—you begin tensing all of your muscles more and more in a desperate attempt to escape. But you cannot do so. Keep trying until you cannot stand it any longer, and then, using a movement that involves your entire body, throw aside the confines of the coffin, breathe deeply, and find yourself free. This movement will have a greater effect if you scream at the same time; it should be a scream that emanates from the depths of your body.

"When we both experienced the love that consumes, we shared in the Absolute. The Absolute shows each of us who we really are; it is an enormous web of cause and effect, where every small gesture made by one person affects the life of someone else. This morning, that slice of the Absolute was still very much alive in my soul. I was seeing not only you but everything there is in the world, unlimited by space or time. Now, the effect is much weaker and will only return in its full strength the next time that I do the exercise of the love that consumes."

I remembered Petrus's bad mood of that morning. If what he said was true, the world was going through a very bad phase.

"I will be waiting for you there at the Parador," he said, as he prepared to leave. "I will leave your name at the desk."

I watched him walk away until I could no longer see him. In the fields to my left, the peasants had finished their day's labors and gone home. I decided that I would do the exercise as soon as darkness had fallen.

I was content. It was the first time I had been completely alone since I had started along the Strange Road to Santiago. I stood up and explored my immediate surroundings, but night was falling fast, and I decided to go back to the tree before I got lost. Before it became completely dark, I made a mental estimate of the distance between the tree and the road. Even in darkness, I would be able to see the way perfectly well and make my way to Santo Domingo with just the help of the frail new moon that had risen in the sky.

Up until that point, I had not been at all frightened; I felt that it would take a lot of imagination to make me fearful of any kind of horrible death. But no matter how long we have lived, when night falls it arouses the hidden fears that have been there in our souls since we were children. The darker it grew, the less comfortable I became.

There I was, alone in the fields; if I were to scream, no one would even hear me. I remembered that I had almost passed out completely that morning. Never in my life had I felt my heart to be so out of control.

And what if I had died? My life would have ended, obviously. Through my experiences with the Tradition, I had already communicated with many spirits. I was absolutely certain that there was a life after death, but it had never occurred to me to wonder just how the transition was made. To pass from one dimension to another, no matter how well prepared one is, must be terrible. If I had died that morning, for example, I would have known nothing else about the rest of the Road to Santiago, about my years of study, about my family's grief for me, or about the money hidden in my belt. I thought about a plant on my desk in Brazil. The plant would go on, as would other plants, as would the streetcars, as would the man on the corner who charges more for his vegetables than anyone else, as would the woman at directory assistance who provides me with telephone numbers that are not listed in the book. All these things—which would have disappeared if I had died that morning—took on an enormous importance for me. I realized that those were the things, rather than the stars or wisdom, that told me I was alive.

The night was quite dark, and on the horizon I could see the faint lights of the city. I lay down on the ground and looked at the branches of the tree overhead. I began to hear strange sounds, sounds of all kinds. They were the sounds of the nocturnal animals, setting out on the hunt. Petrus could not know everything; he was just another human being like me. How was I to know if his guarantee about the absence of poisonous snakes was true? And the wolves, those eternal European wolves—wasn't it possible that they had decided to show up there that night, sniffing out my presence?

A louder noise, similar to the breaking of a branch, frightened me, and my heart once again started pounding.

I was growing scared. The best thing to do would be to complete the exercise right away and then head for the hotel. I began to relax and crossed my arms over my chest in the posture of death. Something nearby made a sound. I jumped up immediately.

It was nothing. The night had aroused my greatest fears. I lay down again, deciding that this time I would turn any source of fear into a stimulus for the exercise. I noticed that even though the temperature had fallen quite a bit, I was perspiring.

I imagined my coffin being closed, and the screws being turned. I was immobile, but I was alive, and I wanted to tell my family that I was seeing everything. I wanted to tell them all that I loved them, but not a sound came out of my mouth. My father and mother were weeping, my wife and my friends were gathered around, but I was completely alone! With all of the people dear to me standing there, no one was able to see that I was alive and that I had not yet accomplished all that I wanted to do in this world. I tried desperately to open my eyes, to give a sign, to beat on the lid of the coffin. But I could not move any part of my body.

I felt the coffin being carried toward the grave. I could hear the sound of the handles grinding against their fittings, the steps of those in the procession, and conversations from this side and that. Someone said that he had a date for dinner later on, and another observed that I had died early. The smell of flowers all around me began to suffocate me.

I remembered how I had given up trying to establish a relationship with two or three women, fearing their rejection. I remembered also the number of times I had failed to do what I wanted to do, thinking I could always do it later. I felt very sorry for myself, not only because I was about to be buried alive but also because I had been afraid to live. Why be fearful of saying no to someone or of leaving something undone when the most important thing of all was to enjoy life fully? There I was, trapped in a coffin, and it was already too late to go back and show the courage I should have had.

There I was, having played the role of my own Judas, having betrayed myself. There I was, powerless to move a muscle, screaming for help, while the others were involved in their lives, worrying about what they were going to do that night, admiring statues and buildings that I would never see again. I began to feel how unfair it was to have to be buried while others continued to live. I would have felt better if there had been a catastrophe and all of us had been in the same boat, heading for the same abyss toward which they were carrying me now. Help! I tried to cry out. I'm still alive. I haven't died. My mind is still functioning!

They placed my coffin at the edge of the grave. They are going to bury me! My wife is going to forget all about me; she will marry someone else and spend the money we have struggled to save for all these years! But who cares about that. I want to be with her now, because I'm alive!

I hear sobs, and I feel tears falling from my eyes, too. If my friends were to open my coffin now, they would see my tears and save me. But instead all I feel is the lowering of the coffin into the ground. Suddenly, everything is dark. A moment ago, there was a ray of light at the edge of the coffin, but now the darkness is complete. The grave diggers' shovels are filling in the grave, and I'm alive! Buried alive! I sense that the air is being cut off, and the fragrance of the flowers is awful. I hear the mourners' departing footsteps.

My terror is total. I'm not able to do anything; if they go away now, it will soon be night, and no one will hear me knocking on the lid of my coffin!

The footsteps fade, nobody hears my screams, and I am alone in the darkness; the air is heavy, and the smell of the flowers is driving me crazy. Suddenly, I hear a sound. It's the worms, coming to eat me alive. I try with all my strength to move the parts of my body, but I am inert. The worms begin to climb over my body. They are sticky and cold. They creep over my face and crawl into my shorts. One of them enters through my anus, and another begins to sneak into a nostril. Help! I'm being eaten alive, and nobody can hear me; nobody says a word to me. The worm that entered my nostril has reached my throat. I feel another invading my ear. I have to get out! Where is God; why doesn't he help me? They are beginning to eat at my throat, and soon I won't be able to scream! They are coming into me everywhere: through my ear, the corner of my mouth, the opening in my penis. I feel those disgusting, oily things inside me, and I have to scream; I have to get away! I am shut up in this cold, dark grave, alone and being eaten alive! The air is giving out, and the worms are eating me! I have to move. I have to break out of this coffin! God, help me gather all of my strength, because I have to escape! I HAVE TO GET OUT OF HERE; I HAVE TO . . . I'M GOING TO GET OUT! I'M GOING TO GET OUT!

I DID IT!

The boards of the coffin flew in all directions, the grave disappeared, and I filled my lungs with the fresh air of the Road to Santiago. My body was trembling from head to foot and bathed in perspiration. I moved a bit and felt that my insides had been twisted around. But none of this was important: I was alive.

The shaking continued, and I made no effort whatsoever to control it. A great sense of calm came over me, and I felt a kind of presence alongside me. I looked over and saw the face of my death. This was not the death that I had experienced a few minutes before, the death I had created with my fears and my imagination; it was my true death, my friend and counselor, who was never again going to allow me to act like such a coward. Starting then, he was going to be of more help to me than Petrus's guiding hand and advice. He was not going to allow me to put off until tomorrow what I should be enjoying today. He was not going to let me flee from life's battles, and he was going to help me fight the good fight. Never again, ever, was I going to feel ridiculous about doing anything. Because he was there, saying that when he took me in hand to travel with me to other worlds, I should leave behind the greatest sin of all: regret. With the certainty of his presence and the gentleness of his face, I was sure that I was going to be able to drink from the fountain of life.

The night held no further secrets or terrors. It was a joyful night, filled with peace. When the trembling ceased, I got up and walked to the pumps in the fields. I washed my shorts and put on a fresh pair from my knapsack. Then I returned to the tree and ate the two sandwiches that Petrus had left for me. They seemed like the most delicious food in the world, because I was alive and because death frightened me no longer.

I decided to sleep right there. The darkness had never been so reassuring.

Personal Vices

We were in the middle of a level field of wheat that stretched all the way to the horizon. The only object that stood out in the scene was another medieval column supporting a cross, one of the road markers for pilgrims. As we approached the column, Petrus stopped, placed his knapsack on the ground, and knelt down. He told me to do the same.

"We are going to say a prayer concerning the only thing that can defeat you as a pilgrim after you find your sword: your personal vices. No matter how much you learn from your Master about how to handle the sword, one of your hands will always be your potential enemy. Let us pray that, if you are successful in finding your sword, you will always wield it with the hand that does not bring scandal down upon you."

It was two o'clock in the afternoon, and there wasn't a sound to be heard as Petrus began to pray aloud:

"Pity us, O Lord, for we are pilgrims on the road to Compostela, and our being here may be a vice. In your infinite pity, help us never to turn our knowledge against ourselves.

"Have pity on those who pity themselves and who see themselves as good people treated unfairly by life—who feel that they do not deserve what has befallen them. Such people will never be able to fight the good fight. And pity those who are cruel to themselves and who see only the evil in their own actions, feeling that they are to blame for the injustice in the world. Because neither of these kinds of people know thy law that says, 'But the very hairs of your head are numbered.'

"Have pity on those who command and those who serve during long hours of work, and who sacrifice themselves in exchange merely for a Sunday off, only to find that there is nowhere to go, and everything is closed. But also have pity on those who sanctify their efforts, and who are able to go beyond the bounds of their own madness, winding up indebted, or nailed to the cross by their very brothers. Because neither of these kinds of people know thy law that says, 'Be ye therefore as wise as the serpents and as harmless as the doves.'

"Have pity on those who may conquer the world but never join the good fight within themselves. But pity also those who have won the good fight within themselves, and now find themselves in the streets and the bars of life because they were unable to conquer the world. Because neither of these kinds of people know thy law that says, 'He who heeds my words I will liken to a wise man who built his house on rock.'

"Have pity on those who are fearful of taking up a pen, or a paintbrush, or an instrument, or a tool because they are afraid that someone has already done so better than they could, and who feel themselves to be unworthy to enter the marvelous mansion of art. But have even more pity on those who, having taken up the pen, or the paintbrush, or the instrument, or the tool, have turned inspiration into a paltry thing, and yet feel themselves to be better than others. Neither of these kinds of people know thy law that says, 'For there is nothing covered that will not be revealed, nor hidden that will not be known.'

"Pity those who eat and drink and sate themselves, but are unhappy and alone in their satiety. But pity even more those who fast, and who censure and prohibit, and who thereby see themselves as saints, preaching your name in the streets. For neither of these types of people know thy law that says, 'If I bear witness of myself, my witness is not true.'

"Pity those who fear death, and are unaware of the many kingdoms through which they have already passed, and the many deaths they have already suffered, and who are unhappy because they think that one day their world will end. But have even more pity for those who already know their many deaths, and today think of themselves as immortal. Neither of these kinds of people know thy law that says, 'Except that one is born again, he cannot see the kingdom of God.'

"Have pity on those who bind themselves with the silken ties of love, and think of themselves as masters of others, and who feel envy, and poison themselves, and who torture themselves because they cannot see that love and all things change like the wind. But pity even more those who die of their fear of loving and who reject love in the name of a greater love that they know not. Neither of these kinds of people know thy law that says, 'Whoever drinks of the water that I shall give him will never thirst.'

"Pity those who reduce the cosmos to an explanation, God to a magic potion, and humanity to beings with basic needs that must be satisfied, because they never hear the music of the spheres. But have even more pity on those who have blind faith, and who in their laboratories transform mercury into gold, and who are surrounded by their books about the secrets of the Tarot and the power of the pyramids. Neither of these kinds of people know thy law that says, 'Whoever does not receive the kingdom of God as a little child will by no means enter it.'

"Pity those who see no one but themselves, and for whom others are a blurred and distant scenario as they pass through the streets in their limousines and lock themselves in their air-conditioned penthouse offices, as they suffer in silence the solitude of power. But pity even more those who will do anything for anybody, and are charitable, and seek to win out over evil only through love. For neither of these kinds of people know thy law that says, 'Let he who has no sword sell his garment and buy one.'

"Have pity, Lord, on we who seek out and dare to take up the sword that you have promised, and who are a saintly and sinful lot scattered throughout the world. Because we do not recognize even ourselves, and often think that we are dressed, but we are nude; we believe that we have committed a crime, when in reality we have saved someone's life. And do not forget in your pity for all of us that we hold the sword with the hand of an angel and the hand of a devil, and that they are both the same hand. Because we are of the world, and we continue to be of the world, and we have need of thee. We will always be in need of thy law that says, 'When I sent you without money bag, knapsack, and sandals, you lacked nothing.'"

Petrus ended his prayer. As silence prevailed, he gazed out over the field of wheat that surrounded us.

Conquest

We arrived one afternoon at the ruins of an old castle of the Order of the Knights Templar. We sat down to rest, and while Petrus smoked his usual cigarette, I drank a bit of the wine left over from lunch. I studied the view that surrounded us: a few peasant houses, the tower of the castle, the undulating fields ready for sowing. To my right appeared a shepherd, guiding his flock past the walls of the castle, bound for home. The sky was red, and the dust raised by the animals blurred the view, making it look like a dream or a magic vision. The shepherd waved to us, and we waved back.

The sheep passed in front of us and continued down the road. Petrus got to his feet. It was an impressive scene, and I would like to have stayed, but Petrus said, "Let's go, right away. We've got to hurry."

"Why?"

"Because I said so. Don't you think we have spent enough time on the Road to Santiago?"

But something told me that his haste had something to do with the magic scene of the shepherd and his sheep.

Two days later we were close to some mountains to the south; their elevation was a relief to the monotony of the immense wheat fields. The area had some natural elevations, but it was well punctuated by the yellow markers that Father Jordi had mentioned. At that point, Petrus, without explanation, began to stray from the markers and to plunge more and more in a northerly direction. When I pointed this out to him, he answered brusquely, saying that he was the guide and that he knew where he was leading me.

After half an hour or so along the new path, I began to hear the sound of tumbling water. All about us were the sun-drenched fields, and I tried to imagine what the sound could be. As we continued, the sound grew louder, and there was no doubt that it was produced by a waterfall. But I could see neither mountains nor falls near us.

Then, as we crested a small rise, we were confronted with one of nature's most extravagant works: a basin opened up in the plateau, deep enough to contain a five-story building, and a stream hurtled to its floor. The immense crater was bordered by luxuriant vegetation, completely different in appearance from the flora we had been passing until then, and it framed the falling water.

"Let's climb down here," Petrus said.

We began a descent that put me in mind of Jules Verne; it was as if we were descending to the center of the earth. The way was steep and difficult to navigate, and so as not to fall, we were forced to grasp at thorny branches and sharp rocks. When I reached the bottom, my arms and legs were lacerated.

"Isn't this beautiful," said Petrus, taking no notice of my discomfort.

I agreed. It was an oasis in the desert. The plant life and the rainbow formed by the droplets of water made the basin as beautiful seen from below as from above.

"This is where nature really shows its power," he said.

"True," I nodded.

"And it gives us a chance to show our own strength. Let's climb the falls," said my guide. "Through the water!"

I looked again at the scene. Now I no longer saw it as an oasis, nor as one of nature's more sophisticated caprices. Instead, I was looking at a wall more than fifty feet high over which the water fell with a deafening force. The small lagoon formed by the cataract was no deeper than a man's height, since the river ran to an opening that probably took it underground. On the wall, there were no protrusions that I could make use of in a climb, and the depth of the pool was not sufficient to break a fall. I was looking at an absolutely impossible task.

I thought of an event from five years ago, during a ritual that had required—like this situation—an extremely dangerous climb. My Master had given me a choice as to whether I wanted to continue or not. I was younger and fascinated by his powers and by the miracles of the Tradition, so I decided to go on. I needed to demonstrate my courage and my bravery.

After I had climbed the mountain for nearly an hour and as I was approaching the most difficult stretch, a wind of unexpected force arose, and to keep myself from falling, I had had to cling with all my strength to the small ledge that supported me. I closed my eyes, expecting the worst, and dug my nails into the rock. A minute later, I was surprised to find that someone had helped me to assume a safer and more comfortable position. I opened my eyes to see that my Master was there at my side.

He made some gestures in the air, and the wind suddenly ceased. With an absolutely mysterious agility, at times seeming to require an exercise in levitation, he descended the mountain and told me to do likewise.

I arrived at the base with my legs trembling and asked him angrily why he hadn't caused the wind to abate before it threatened me.

"Because it was I who ordered the wind to blow," he answered.

"So it would kill me?"

"No, in order to save you. It would have been impossible for you to climb this mountain. When I asked if you wanted to, I was not testing your courage. I was testing your wisdom.

"You made it into an order, when I had not given one," said the Master. "If you were able to levitate yourself, you would not have had a problem. But you wanted to be brave, when it was enough to have been intelligent."

That day, he told me about Magi who had become insane during the process of illumination and who could no longer distinguish between their own powers and those of their disciples. During my lifetime, I have known some great men in the Tradition. I had gotten to know three great Masters—including my own—who were able to dominate material objects in ways that went far beyond what anyone could imagine. I had witnessed miracles, exact predictions of the future, and knowledge of past incarnations. My Master had spoken of the Falklands War two months before Argentina had invaded the islands. He had described everything in detail and had explained the reasons, on an astral level, for the conflict.

But after that day, I had begun to notice that there were Magi who, in the Master's words, had been "crazed by the process of illumination." They were individuals who in almost every way were the equal of their Masters, even with respect to their powers: I saw one of them make a seed germinate in twenty minutes of extreme concentration. But that man and some others had already led many disciples to madness and despair; some of those disciples had had to be committed to mental hospitals, and there was at least one confirmed case of suicide. Those Masters were on the "blacklist" of the Tradition, but it was impossible to control them, and I know that many of them continue their work even today.

All of this passed through my mind in a fraction of a second as I looked at the waterfall that seemed impossible to scale. I thought of the length of time that Petrus and I had traveled together, of the dog's attack that had left me unhurt, of Petrus's lack of control with the boy who had waited on us in the restaurant, and of Petrus's drinking bout at the wedding celebration. Those events were all I could remember.

"Petrus, there's no way I'm going to climb that waterfall. And for a very simple reason: it's impossible."

He didn't say a word. He sat down in the grass, and I did the same. We sat there in silence for fifteen minutes. His silence disarmed me, and I took the initiative by beginning to speak.

"Petrus, I don't want to climb because I'll fall. I know that I'm not going to die, because when I saw the face of my death, I also saw the day it will happen. But I could fall and be crippled for the rest of my life."

"Paulo, Paulo . . ." He looked at me and smiled. "You have completely changed. There is in your voice a bit of the love that consumes, and your eyes are shining."

"Are you going to say that I'm breaking a vow of obedience that I made before setting out on the Road?"

"You are not breaking that vow. You are not afraid, and you are not lazy. Nor should you be thinking that I have given you a useless order. You don't want to climb the falls because you are thinking about the Black Magi.[1] You have

[1]This is the name given, in the Tradition, to those Masters who have lost their magical contact with their disciples, as just described. This expression is also used to describe Masters who interrupted their learning process after having established dominion only over earthly forces.

not broken a vow just because you have used your decision-making ability. A pilgrim is never prevented from using that ability."

I looked again at the cataract and again at Petrus. I was weighing my chances of success in making the climb, and they didn't weigh very much.

"Now, pay attention," he continued. "I'm going to climb before you do, without using any gift. And I'm going to make it. If I succeed just by knowing where to place my feet, you will have to climb, too. I am nullifying your freedom to make a decision. If you refuse, after you have seen me make the climb, then you will be breaking your vow."

Petrus began to take off his sneakers. He was at least ten years older than I, and if he succeeded in the climb, I would have no further excuse. I studied the waterfall and felt my stomach seize up.

But he didn't move. Even though he had taken off his sneakers, he remained seated in the same place. He looked at the sky and said, "A few kilometers from here, in 1502, the Virgin appeared to a shepherd. Today is the feast day commemorating that event—the Feast of the Virgin of the Road—and I am going to offer my victory to her. I would advise you to do the same thing. Offer a victory to her. Don't offer the pain in your feet or the cuts on your hands from the rocks. Everybody in the world offers only pain as penance. There is nothing wrong with that, but I think she would be happier if, rather than just pain, people would also offer her their joys."

I was in no condition to speak. I still doubted whether Petrus could climb the wall. I thought the whole thing was a farce, that I was being drawn in by the way he spoke and that he would then convince me to do something I really did not want to do. In the face of these doubts, I closed my eyes for a moment and prayed to the Virgin of the Road. I promised that if Petrus and I were able to climb the wall, I would one day return to this place.

"Everything you have learned up to now makes sense only if it is applied in real life. Don't forget that I described the Road to Santiago to you as the road of the common person; I have said that a thousand times. On the Road to Santiago and in life itself, wisdom has value only if it helps us to overcome some obstacle.

"A hammer would make no sense in the world if there were not nails to be driven. And even given the existence of nails, the hammer would be useless if it only thought, 'I can drive those nails with two blows.' The hammer has to act. To put itself into the hands of the carpenter and to be used in its proper function."

I remembered my Master's words at Itatiaia: "Whoever has the sword must constantly put it to the test, so it doesn't rust in its scabbard."

"The waterfall is the place where you will put into practice everything you have learned so far," said my guide. "There is one thing working in your favor: you know the day on which you are going to die so that fear will not paralyze you when you have to decide quickly where to find a hold. But remember that you are going to have to work with the water and use it to provide what you need. Remember that you have to dig a nail into your thumb if a bad thought takes over. And most important, that you have to find support for yourself in the love that consumes during every minute of the climb, because it is that love which directs and justifies your every step."

Petrus fell silent. He took off his shirt and his shorts and was completely naked. He went into the cold water of the lagoon, wet himself completely, and spread his arms to the sky. I could see that he was happy; he was enjoying the coldness of the water and the rainbows created by the mist that surrounded us.

"One more thing," he said, before going in under the falls. "This waterfall will teach you how to be a Master. I am going to make the climb, but there will be a veil of water between you and me. I will climb without your being able to see where I place my hands and feet.

"In the same way, a disciple such as you can never imitate his guide's steps. You have your own way of living your life, of dealing with problems, and of winning. Teaching is only demonstrating that it is possible. Learning is making it possible for yourself."

He said nothing else as he disappeared through the veil of the cascade and began to climb. I could see only his outline, as if perceived through frosted glass. But I could see that he was climbing. Slowly and inexorably he moved toward the top. The closer he got to the crest, the more fearful I became, because my time was coming. Finally, the most terrible moment arrived: the moment when he had to come up through the falling water without holding to the sides. The force of the water would surely plunge him back to the ground. But Petrus's head emerged there at the top, and the falling water became his silver mantle. I saw him for just an instant because, with a rapid motion, he threw his body upward and secured himself somehow on top of the plateau, still immersed in the stream of water. Then, I lost sight of him for some moments.

Finally, Petrus appeared on the bank. He was bathed in moisture, brilliant in the sunlight, and laughing.

"Let's go," he yelled, waving his hands. "It's your turn."

It really was my turn. Either I did it, or I forever renounced my sword.

I took all of my clothes off and prayed again to the Virgin of the Road. Then I dived into the lagoon. It was freezing, and my body went rigid with its impact; but I then felt a pleasant sensation, a sensation of being really alive. Without thinking about it, I went straight to the waterfall.

The weight of the water on my head brought me back to a sense of reality, the sense that weakens us at the moment when we most need to have faith in our powers. I could see that the falls had much more force than I had thought and that if the water continued to fall directly onto the top of my head, it would defeat me, even if I kept both feet firmly planted on the bottom of the lagoon. I passed through the falls and stood between the water and the rock, in a space into which my body just fit, glued to the wall. From there, I could see that the task was easier than I had thought.

The water did not beat down here, and what had appeared to me to be a wall with a polished surface was actually a wall with a great many cavities. I was dumbfounded to think that I might have renounced my sword out of fear of the smoothness of the wall when it turned out to be the kind of rock that I had climbed dozens of times. I seemed to hear Petrus's voice saying, "Didn't I tell you? Once a problem is solved, its simplicity is amazing."

I began to climb, with my face against the humid rock. In ten minutes I was almost to the top. Only one hurdle remained: the final phase, the place where the water fell over the crest on its trajectory toward the lagoon. The victory I had won in making the climb would be worth nothing if I were not able to negotiate the last stretch that separated me from the open air. This was where the danger lay, and I had not been able to see how Petrus had succeeded. I prayed again to the Virgin of the Road, a Virgin I had never heard of but who was now the object of all my faith and all my hopes for success. I began tentatively to put first my hair and then my entire head up through the water that was rushing over and past me.

The water covered me completely and blurred my vision. I began to feel its impact and held firmly to the rock. I bent my head to create an air pocket that would allow me to breathe. I trusted completely in my hands and feet. My hands had, after all, already held an ancient sword, and my feet had trod the Road to Santiago. They were my friends, and they were helping me. But the noise of the water was deafening, and I began to have trouble breathing. I was determined to put my head through the flow, and for several seconds everything went black. I fought with all my strength to keep my hands and feet anchored to their holds, but the noise of the water seemed to take me to another place. It was a mysterious and distant place where nothing that was happening at that moment was at all important, and it was a place that I could get to if I had the strength. In that place, there would no longer be any need for the superhuman effort it took to keep my hands and feet holding to the rock; there would be only rest and peace.

But my hands and feet did not obey this impulse to surrender. They had resisted a mortal temptation. And my head began to emerge from the stream as gradually as it had entered it. I was overcome by a profound love for my body. It was there, helping me in this crazy adventure of climbing through a waterfall in search of a sword.

When my head came completely through the surface, I saw the bright sun above me and took a deep breath. This renewed my strength, and as I looked about, I could see, just a few inches away, the plateau we had originally walked along—the end of the journey. I had an impulse to throw myself up and grab for something to hold, but I could see nothing to grab through the flowing water. The impulse was strong, but the moment of victory had not yet come, and I had to control myself. I was at the most difficult point in the ascent, with the water beating on my chest, and the pressure was

146

threatening to throw me back to the place below that I had dared to leave in pursuit of my dream.

It was no time to be thinking about Masters or friends, and I could not look to the side to see if Petrus would be able to save me if I should slip. "He has probably made this climb a million times," I thought, "and he knows that here is where I most desperately need help." But he had abandoned me. Or maybe he hadn't abandoned me, but he was there somewhere behind me, and I couldn't turn to look for him without losing my balance. I had to do it all. I, alone, had to win my victory.

I kept my feet and one hand holding to the rock, while the other hand let go and sought to become one with the water. I didn't want to exert any more effort, because I was already using all of my strength. My hand, knowing this, became a fish that gives itself up but knows where it wants to go. I remembered films from my childhood in which I had seen salmon jumping over waterfalls because they had a goal and they simply had to achieve it.

The arm rose slowly, using the force of the water to its advantage. It finally burst free, and it took on the task of finding a hold and deciding the fate of the rest of my body. Like a salmon in the film, the hand dived into the water atop the crest, searching for a place, a point that would support me in the final leap.

The rock had been polished by centuries of running water. But there must be a handhold: if Petrus had been able to find one, I could, too. I began to feel great pain, because now I knew that I was only one step from success; this is the moment when one's strength begins to flag, and one loses confidence in oneself. On a few occasions in my life I had lost at the last minute—swum across an ocean and drowned in the surf of regret. But I was on the Road to Santiago, and that old experience must not be allowed to repeat itself—I had to win.

My free hand slid along the smooth stone, and the pressure was becoming stronger and stronger. I felt that my other limbs could not hold out and that I was going to begin to cramp. The water was beating on my genitals, too, and the pain was unbearable. Then my free hand suddenly found a hold in the rock. It wasn't a large one, and it was off to the side of where I wanted to rise, but it would serve as a support for my other hand when its turn came. I marked its location mentally, and my free hand returned to its search for my salvation. A few inches from the first hold, I found another.

There it was! There was the place that for centuries had served as a hold for the pilgrims bound for Santiago. I could see this, and I held on with all my strength. The other hand came free, was thrown back by the force of the water, but, in an arc across the sky, reached and found the handhold. With a quick movement, my entire body followed the path opened by my arms, and I threw myself upward.

The biggest and final step had been taken. My whole body came up through the water, and a moment later the savage waterfall had become just a trickle of water, hardly moving. I crawled to the bank and gave in to exhaustion. The sun fell on my body, warming me, and I told myself again that I had won, that I was alive as before when I had stood below in the lagoon. Over the sound of the water, I heard Petrus's approaching footsteps.

I wanted to get up and show how happy I was, but my exhausted body refused.

"Relax, rest a little," he said. "Try to breathe slowly."

I did so and fell into a deep, dreamless sleep. When I awoke, the sun had moved across the sky, and Petrus, already fully dressed, handed me my clothes and said we had to move on.

"I'm very tired," I answered.

"Don't worry. I am going to show you how to draw energy from everything around you."

And Petrus taught me the RAM Breathing Exercise.

I did the exercise for five minutes and felt better. I arose, dressed, and grabbed my knapsack.

"Come here," Petrus said. I went to the edge of the cliff. At my feet, the waterfall rushed by.

"Looking at it from here, it looks a lot easier than it did from down there," I said.

"Exactly. And if I had shown it to you from here before, you would have been misled. You would have made a poor analysis of your chances."

I still felt weak, and I repeated the exercise. Shortly, the entire universe about me fell into harmony with me and came into my heart. I asked Petrus why he had not taught me RAM breathing before, since many times I had felt lazy and tired on the Road to Santiago.

"Because you never looked like you felt that way," he said, laughing. Then he asked me if I still had any of the delicious butter cookies I had bought in Astorga.

THE RAM BREATHING EXERCISE

Expel all of the air from your lungs, emptying them as much as you can. Then, inhale slowly as you raise your arms as high as possible. As you inhale, concentrate on allowing love, peace, and harmony with the universe to enter into your body.

Hold the air you have taken in and keep your arms raised for as long as you can, enjoying the harmony between your inner sensations and the outer world. When you reach your limit, exhale all of the air rapidly, as you say the word, "RAM."

Repeat this process for five minutes each time you do the exercise.

Madness

For three days we had been making a kind of forced march. Petrus would wake me before daybreak, and we would not end our day's hike before nine in the evening. The only rest stops granted were for quick meals, since my guide had abolished our siesta. He gave the impression that he was keeping to some mysterious schedule that he hadn't shared with me.

What's more, his behavior had changed completely. At first, I thought it had something to do with my hesitation at the waterfall, but later I could see that it was not that. He was irritable with everyone, and he looked at his watch frequently during the day. I reminded him that it was he who had told me that we ourselves create the pace of time.

"You are becoming wiser every day," he answered. "Let's see if you can put all of this wisdom into play when it is needed."

On one afternoon, I was so tired from the pace of our hiking that I simply could not get up. Petrus told me to take my shirt off and settle my spine along the trunk of a nearby tree. I held that position for several minutes and felt much better. He began to explain to me that vegetation, and especially mature trees, are able to transmit harmony when one rests one's nerve centers against a tree trunk. For hours he discoursed on the physical, energetic, and spiritual properties of plants.

Since I had already read all of this somewhere, I didn't worry about taking notes. But Petrus's discourse helped to diminish my feeling that he was irritated with me. Afterward, I treated his silence with greater respect, and he, perhaps guessing correctly at my apprehension, tried to be friendlier whenever his constant bad mood allowed him to do so.

We arrived one morning at an immense bridge, totally out of proportion to the modest stream that coursed below it. It was early on a Sunday morning, and, since the bars and taverns nearby were all closed, we sat down there to eat our breakfast.

"People and nature are equally capricious," I said, trying to start a conversation. "We build beautiful bridges, and then Mother Nature changes the course of the rivers they cross."

"It's the drought," he said. "Finish your sandwich, because we have to move along."

I decided to ask him why we were in such a hurry.

"We have been on the Road to Santiago for a long time. I have already told you that I left a lot of things unattended in Italy, and I have got to get back."

I wasn't convinced. What he was saying might well be true, but it wasn't the only issue. When I started to question what he had said, he changed the subject.

"What do you know about this bridge?"

"Nothing," I answered. "But even with the drought, it's too big. I think the river must have changed its course."

"As far as that goes, I have no idea," he said. "But it is known along the Road to Santiago as the 'honorable passage.' These fields around us were the site of some bloody battles between the Suevians and the Visigoths, and later between Alphonse III's soldiers and the Moors. Maybe the bridge is oversize to allow all that blood to run past without flooding the city."

He was making an attempt at macabre humor. I didn't laugh, and he was put off for a moment, but then he continued, "However, it wasn't the Visigoth hordes or the triumphant cries of Alphonse III that gave this bridge its name. It was another story of love and death.

"During the first centuries of the Road to Santiago, pilgrims, priests, nobles, and even kings came from all over Europe to pay homage to the saint. Because of this, there was also an influx of assailants and robbers. History has recorded innumerable cases of robbery of entire caravans of pilgrims and of horrible crimes committed against lone travelers."

Just like today, I thought.

"Because of the crimes, some of the nobility decided to provide protection for the pilgrims, and each of the nobles involved took responsibility for protecting one segment of the Road. But just as rivers change their course, people's ideals are subject to alteration. In addition to frightening the malefactors, the knights began to compete with each other to determine who was the strongest and most courageous on the Road. It wasn't long before they began to do battle with each other, and the bandits returned to the Road with impunity.

"This developed over a long period of time until, in 1434, a noble from the city of León fell in love with a woman. The man was Don Suero de Quiñones; he was powerful and rich, and he did everything in his power to win his lady's hand in marriage. But this woman—history has forgotten her name— did not even want to know about his grand passion and rejected his request."

I was dying of curiosity to know what an unrequited love had to do with battles among the knights. Petrus saw that I was interested and said that he would relate the rest of the story only if I finished my sandwich and we began to move along.

"You are just like my mother when I was a child," I said. But I gulped down the last morsel of bread, picked up my knapsack, and we began to make our way through the sleepy city.

Petrus continued, "Our gentleman, whose pride had been offended, resolved to do what all men do when they feel themselves to have been rejected: he began a private war. He promised himself that he was going to perform such an important feat that the woman would never forget his name. For months he sought a noble idea that would consecrate his spurned love. And then he heard of the crimes and the battles along the Road to Santiago. That gave him an idea.

"He called together ten of his friends, and they set themselves up in the small city we are passing through right now. He spread the word by means of the pilgrims that he was prepared to remain there for thirty days—and break thirty lances—in order to prove that he was the strongest and boldest of all the knights of the Road. He established himself with his banners, his standards, his pages, and servants, and waited for challengers."

I could imagine what a picnic that must have been: roast boar, endless supplies of wine, music, stories, and battles. A lively picture came to my mind as Petrus related the rest of the story.

"The bouts began on the tenth of July with the arrival of the first challengers. Quiñones and his companions fought during the day and held huge feasts every night. The contests were always held on the bridge so that no one could flee. During one period, so many challengers came that fires were built along the entire length of the bridge so that the bouts could go on until dawn. All of the vanquished knights were

154

required to swear that they would never again do battle with the others and that from then on, their only mission would be to protect the pilgrims going to Compostela.

"On the ninth of August, the combat ended, and Don Suero de Quiñones was recognized as the bravest and most valiant of all the knights of the Road to Santiago. From that day forward, no one dared to issue challenges of bravery, and the nobles returned to their battle against the only enemy in common, the bandits who assaulted the pilgrims. This epic was later to give rise to the Military Order of Santiago of the Sword."

We had crossed the small city. I wanted to go back and take another look at the "honorable passage," the bridge on which all of that had taken place. But Petrus said that we had to move on.

"And what happened to Don Quiñones?" I asked.

"He went to Santiago de Compostela and placed a golden necklace at San Tiago's shrine; even today it adorns the bust of San Tiago the Lesser."

"I was asking whether he wound up marrying the lady."

"Oh, I don't know," Petrus answered. "In those days, history was written only by men. With such a battlefield close at hand, who was going to be interested in a love story?"

After telling me the story of Don Suero de Quiñones, my guide went back to his now-habitual silence, and we went along for two more days without a word. We hardly stopped to rest. On the third day, though, Petrus began to walk more slowly than usual. He said that he was a bit tired from the efforts of the week and that he was too old to continue at that pace. Again I was sure that he was not telling the truth; his face, rather than showing fatigue, revealed an intense preoccupation, as if something very important was about to occur.

We arrived that afternoon at Foncebadon, a large village that was completely in ruins. The houses, built of stone, had slate roofs that had been destroyed by time and the rotting of the wood that supported them. One side of the village gave onto a precipice, and in front of us, behind a mountain peak, was one of the most important landmarks of the Road to Santiago: the Iron Cross. This time it was I who was impatient; I wanted to get to that strange monument, comprised of an immense wooden base, almost thirty feet tall, topped by the Iron Cross. The cross had been left there during the epoch of Caesar's invasion, in homage to Mercury. Observing the pagan tradition, the pilgrims along the Jacobean route were accustomed to leaving stones brought from elsewhere at the base of the cross. I took advantage of the abundance of stones in the abandoned village and picked up a piece of slate.

It was only when I had resolved to move along more quickly that I saw that Petrus was walking more slowly. He examined the ruined houses and the fallen tree trunks and finally decided to sit down in the middle of one of the plazas where there was a wooden cross.

"Let's rest a bit," he said.

It was early afternoon, so even if we stayed there for an hour there would still be time to reach the Iron Cross before nightfall.

I sat down beside him and gazed at the empty surroundings. Just as rivers change their course, humans also change where they live. The houses were solid and must have lasted for a long time before falling into ruin. It was a pretty place, with mountains in the distance and a valley in front of us. I asked myself what could have happened to cause the people to leave such a place.

"Do you think that Don Suero de Quiñones was crazy?" Petrus asked.

I did not even remember who Don Suero was, and he had to remind me about the "honorable passage."

"I don't think he was crazy," I answered. But I wasn't sure about my answer.

"Well, he was, just as Alfonso, the monk that you met, was. Just as I am, as you can see from the plans that I make. Or you, seeking your sword. Every one of us has the flame of madness burning inside, and it is fed by agape.

"Crazy doesn't mean you want to conquer America or talk to the birds like Saint Francis of Assisi. Even a vegetable vendor on the street corner can show this flame of madness if he likes what he is doing. Agape is grander than our ordinary human concepts, and everyone thirsts for it."

Petrus told me that I knew how to invoke agape by means of the Blue Sphere Exercise. But in order for agape to flourish, I must not be afraid to change my life. If I liked what I was doing, very well. But if I did not, there was always the time for a change. If I allowed change to occur, I would be transforming myself into a fertile field and allowing the Creative Imagination to sow its seeds in me.

"Everything I have taught you, including agape, makes sense only if you are satisfied with yourself. If you are not, then the exercises you have learned are inevitably going to make you seek change. And if you do not want all of those exercises to work against you, you have to allow change to happen.

"This is the most difficult moment in a person's life—when the person witnesses the good fight and is unable to change and join the battle. When this happens, knowledge turns against the person who holds it."

I looked at the deserted city of Foncebadon. Maybe all of those people, collectively, had felt the need for a change. I asked whether Petrus had chosen this place purposely in order to say all of this to me.

"I don't know what happened here," he answered. "Often people have to accept the changes that destiny forces upon them, but that's not what I'm talking about. I am speaking of an act of will, a concrete desire to do battle against everything that is unsatisfying in one's everyday life.

"On the road of our lives, we always run into problems that are hard to solve—like, for example, passing through a waterfall without letting it make us fall. So you have to allow the Creative Imagination to do its work. In your case, the waterfall was a life-and-death situation, and there wasn't time to consider many options; agape showed you the only way.

"But there are problems in our lives that require us to choose between one way and another. Everyday problems, like a business decision, the breakup of a relationship, a social obligation. Each of these small decisions we have to make, throughout our lives, might represent a choice between life and death. When you leave the house in the morning on your way to work, you might choose one means of transportation that will drop you off safe and sound or another that is going to crash and kill its passengers. This is a radical example of how a simple decision may affect us for the rest of our lives."

I began to think about myself as Petrus spoke. I had chosen to walk the Road to Santiago in search of my sword. It was the sword that was most important to me now, and I needed somehow to find it. I had to make the right decision.

"The only way to make the right decision is to know what the wrong decision is," he said after I had mentioned my concern. "You have to examine the other path, without fear and without being morbid, and then decide."

It was then that Petrus taught me the Shadows Exercise.

"Your problem is your sword," he said after he had explained the exercise.

I agreed.

158

THE SHADOWS EXERCISE

Relax completely.

For five minutes, study the shadows of all of the objects and people around you. Try to identify exactly which part of the object or person is casting a shadow.

For the next five minutes, continue to do this, but at the same time, focus on the problem you are trying to solve. Look for all of the possible wrong solutions to the problem.

Finally, spend five more minutes studying the shadows and thinking about what correct solutions remain. Eliminate them, one by one, until only the single correct solution is left.

"So do the exercise now. I'm going to take a walk. When I come back, I know that you will have the right solution."

I remembered how much of a hurry Petrus had been in during the past few days, yet now we were having a prolonged conversation in this abandoned city. It seemed to me that he was trying to gain some time so that he, too, could make a decision regarding something. This made me excited, and I began to do the exercise.

I did a bit of RAM breathing to put me in harmony with my surroundings. Then I noted on my watch when fifteen minutes would have passed, and I began to look at the shadows all around me—shadows of ruined houses, stones, wood, and the cross behind me. As I studied the shadows, I saw that it was difficult to know exactly what part was casting any given shadow. I had never noticed this before. Some house beams that were straight were transformed into shadows with sharp angles, and an irregular stone cast a shadow with a smoothly rounded form. I did this for ten minutes. The exercise was so fascinating that it was not difficult to concentrate on it. Then I began to think of the wrong solutions to the problem of finding my sword. Many ideas came to mind—I thought about taking a bus to Santiago, and then I thought about phoning my wife and using some sort of emotional trickery to find out where she had placed it.

When Petrus returned, I was smiling.

"So?" he asked.

"I found out how Agatha Christie wrote her mystery novels," I joked. "She transformed the hunch that was most wrong into the one that was correct. She must have known about the Exercise of the Shadows."

Petrus asked where my sword was.

"First I'm going to tell you the most erroneous guess that I came up with as I looked at the shadows: that the sword is somewhere other than on the Road to Santiago."

"You are a genius. You figured out that we have been walking all this way in order to find your sword. I thought they had told you that already in Brazil."

"It's being kept in a safe place that my wife could not enter," I continued. "I deduced that it's in an absolutely open place but that it has been assimilated so well into its surroundings that it can't be seen."

This time Petrus didn't smile. I went on:

"And since the most absurd thing would be that it is in a place where there are lots of people, it has to be in some locale that is practically deserted. And most important, and so that the few people who see it don't notice the difference between it and a typical Spanish sword, it must be in a place where no one knows how to distinguish between styles of swords."

"Do you think it is here?" he asked.

"No, it's not here. The thing that would be most wrong would be to do this exercise at the place where my sword is. I discarded that hunch right away. It must be in a city that is similar to this one, but it cannot be in an abandoned city, because a sword in an abandoned city would attract a lot of attention from pilgrims and passersby. It would wind up as a decoration on the wall of a bar."

"Very good," he said, and I could see that he was proud of me—or of the exercise he had taught me.

"There's another thing," I said.

"What's that?"

"The place that would be most wrong for the sword of a Magus to be left is a profane place. It has to be in a sacred place. Like a church, for example, where no one would dare to steal it. So, in a church in a small city near Santiago, visible to everyone but embedded in its surroundings—that's where my sword is. Starting now, I'm going to visit every church on the Road."

"You don't have to," he said. "When the moment comes, you will know it."

I had been right!

"Listen, Petrus, why did we hurry for such a long while, when now we're spending so much time in this abandoned city?"

"What would be the answer that is most wrong?"

I glanced at the shadows. He was right. We were there for some reason.

The sun was hidden behind the mountain, but nightfall was still some hours away. I was thinking that the sun was probably shining just then on the Iron Cross. The cross was only a few hundred yards distant, and I really wanted to see it. I also wanted to know why we were waiting around. We had moved along so rapidly for the entire week, and now it seemed to me that the only reason for that must have been that we had to be at this place, on this day, and at this time.

I tried to make conversation to pass the time, but I could see that Petrus was tense and preoccupied. I had already seen Petrus in a bad mood many times, but I could not remember having seen him so tense. And then I remembered that I *had* seen him like this once. It was at breakfast one morning in a small town whose name I could not remember, just before we had run into . . .

I looked to my left. There he was: the dog! The ferocious dog that had thrown me to the ground, the coward of a dog that had immediately fled afterward. Petrus had promised to help me if we ran into him again, and I turned to my guide. But he had disappeared.

I kept my gaze fixed on the dog's eyes while I frantically tried to think of a way to deal with the situation. Neither of us moved, and I was reminded for a moment of the duel scenes in the ghost towns of Western movies. In those films, no one would ever have dreamed of pitting a man against a dog; it just wouldn't have worked. Yet here I was, confronted with a reality that fiction would have considered too far out.

And there was Legion, so named because he was so many. Nearby stood a deserted house. If I were to bolt suddenly, I could climb to its roof, and Legion could not follow. It seemed absurd that I felt trapped by the physical presence of a dog and all that his presence implied.

As I kept my eyes on him, I immediately rejected the possibility of taking flight. Many times along the Road I had feared this moment, and now here it was. Before I could find my sword, I had to meet with the Enemy and either vanquish him or be defeated by him. I had no choice but to go up against him. If I fled now, I would be falling into a trap. It might be that the dog would not appear again, but I would travel the Road to Santiago de Compostela gripped by fear and apprehension. Ever afterward, I would dream about the dog, fearing his reappearance at any minute and living with dread for the rest of my life.

As I thought about all this, the dog started toward me. I stopped thinking immediately and concentrated only on the battle that was about to begin. Petrus had left, and I was alone. I was frightened. And as I experienced that fear, the dog began to move closer, making a low growling sound. The growl was much more threatening than a loud bark would have been, and I became even more terrified. Seeing the weakness in my eyes, the dog leapt on me.

It was as if a boulder had been thrown at my chest. I fell to the ground, and he began to bite at me. I remembered vaguely that I already knew about my death and that it was not to be like this, but even so, my fear grew, and I was unable to control it. I began to fight just to protect my face and throat. An intense pain in my leg caused me to curl up, and I could see that some flesh had been torn away. I took my hands from my head and throat, reaching toward the wound. The dog, seeing this, began an assault on my face. At that moment, one of my hands felt a rock at my side. I grasped it and began to beat on the dog with all my strength.

He backed off a bit, more surprised than hurt, and I was able to stand. The dog continued to retreat, and the bloody stone gave me courage. I was paying too much respect to the strength of my enemy, and this was a trap. He could not be any stronger than I. He might be more agile, but he could not be stronger, because I weighed more and was taller than he. My fear had lessened, but I wasn't in control of myself yet, and with the rock in my hand, I began to shout at the dog. He withdrew a little further and then suddenly stopped.

It seemed as if he were reading my mind. In my desperation I was beginning to feel strong, and I began to think that it was ridiculous to be fighting a dog. A sense of power suddenly came to me, and a hot wind began to blow across the deserted city. Then I began to be tired of the whole thing; when all was said and done, I had only to batter him once on the head with the stone, and I would have won. I wanted it to be over immediately so that I could dress my wound and put an end to this absurd business of swords and the Strange Road to Santiago.

But this was another trap. The dog hurled himself at me and again pushed me to the ground. This time he evaded the rock easily, biting my hand and causing me to let it go. I began to punch him with my hands, but I was not causing any serious damage. The only thing my blows accomplished was to keep him from biting me even more. His sharp claws began to tear my clothing and my arms, and I saw that it was only a matter of time before he took charge completely.

All of a sudden, I heard a voice from within me. The voice said that if the dog established dominion over me, the fight would be over, and I would be saved: defeated but alive. My leg was aching, and my entire body stung from its lacerations.

The voice insisted that I give up, and I recognized whose voice it was: it was Astrain, my messenger, speaking to me. The dog stopped for a moment, as if he had heard the same voice, and once again I felt like leaving the whole thing behind. Astrain had told me in our conversations that many people fail to find the sword in their lives, and what difference did it make? What I wanted to do was go home, be with my wife, have my children, and work at what I liked. Enough of these absurdities, fighting with dogs and climbing waterfalls. This was the second time that this thought had come to me, but the desire to give up was even stronger now, and I was certain that I would surrender.

A sound from the streets of the abandoned city caught the animal's attention. I looked in the direction of the sound and saw a shepherd returning from the fields with his flock. I remembered that I had seen this scene before, in the ruins of an old castle. When the dog spotted the sheep, he jumped away from me and made ready to attack them. This was my salvation.

The shepherd started to yell, and the sheep scattered. Before the dog got completely away, I decided to engage him for another moment or two, just to provide enough time for the animals to flee. I grabbed one of the dog's legs. I had the absurd hope that the shepherd might come to my assistance, and for a moment, my hopes about the sword and the power of RAM returned.

The dog tried to pull away from me. I was no longer the enemy; I was a hindrance. What he wanted now was there in front of him: the sheep. But I continued to grasp the animal's leg, awaiting a shepherd who would not come and suddenly hoping that the sheep would *not* take flight.

That is what saved my soul. An immense feeling of strength infused me. It was no longer the illusion of power, which causes one to become weary of the battle and to want to give in. Astrain whispered to me again, but this time it was something different. He said that I should always confront the world with the same weapons that were used to challenge me. And that I could confront a dog only by transforming myself into a dog.

This was the same craziness that Petrus had talked about that day. I began to feel that I was a dog. I bared my teeth and sounded a low growl, and hatred flowed from the sounds I made. I saw the frightened face of the shepherd off to the side and could sense that the sheep were as terrified of me as they were of the dog.

Legion also saw this and became fearful. Then I attacked him. It was the first time I had done this in our fight. I attacked him with my teeth and my nails, trying to bite the dog in the throat, exactly as I had feared he would do to me. Inside, I felt only a tremendous desire for victory. Nothing else was important. I threw myself on top of the animal and pressed him to the ground. He fought to free himself from the weight of my body, and he clawed at my skin, but I too was biting and scratching. I could sense that if he got out from under me, he would run away, and I did not want that to happen ever again. Today I was going to beat him.

The animal began to show fear in his eyes. Now I was the dog, and he seemed to have been transformed into a man. My old fear was operating in him now. It was so strong that he was able to work his way out from under me, but I corralled him in the basement of one of the abandoned houses. Behind its low slate wall was the precipice, and he had no escape. Right there, he was going to see the face of his death.

I suddenly began to realize that there was something wrong. My thinking was becoming cloudy, and I began to see a gypsy's face with vague images dancing around it. I had turned myself into Legion. This was the source of my power.

The many devils had abandoned the poor, frightened dog that a moment from now was going to fall into an abyss, and now they were in me. I felt a terrible desire to destroy the defenseless animal. "You are the Prince, and they are Legion," whispered Astrain. But I did not want to be a Prince, and I heard from a distance the voice of my Master. He said insistently that there was a sword to be won. I had to resist for one more minute. I should not kill that dog.

I looked over at the shepherd. His look confirmed what I was thinking. He, too, was now more frightened of me than of the dog.

I began to feel dizzy, and the scene began to spin. I could not allow myself to faint. If I fainted now, Legion would have won. I had to find a solution. I was no longer fighting against an animal but against the force that possessed me. I felt my legs beginning to weaken, and I leaned against a wall, but it gave way under my weight. Among the stones and bits of wood, I fell with my face in the dirt.

The earth. Legion was the earth and the fruits of the earth—the good fruits of the earth and the bad, but of the earth. His house was in the earth, and there he ruled the earth or was ruled by it. Agape exploded within me, and I dug my nails into the earth. I screamed, and the scream was the same as I had heard the first time the dog and I had met. I felt Legion pass through my body and descend into the earth. Within me was agape, and Legion did not want to be eaten by the love that consumes. This was my will, the will that had made me fight with my remaining strength against fainting; it was the will of agape residing in my soul and resisting. My entire body trembled.

Legion plummeted into the earth. I began to vomit, but I felt that it was agape, growing and exiting through all of my pores. My body continued to tremble, and a long time later I sensed that Legion had returned to his realm.

I could feel his last vestige pass out through my fingers. I sat on the ground, wounded and exhausted, and looked at the absurd scene in front of me: a dog, bleeding and waving his tail, and a terrified shepherd staring at me.

"It must have been something you ate," said the shepherd, not wanting to believe what he had seen. "But now that you've vomited, you will feel better."

I nodded my head. He thanked me for having controlled "my" dog and went his way down the road with his sheep.

Petrus appeared but said nothing. He tore off a strip of his shirt and made a tourniquet for my leg, which was bleeding badly. He told me to check the rest of my body, and I replied that there was nothing serious.

"You look awful," he said, smiling. His good mood seemed to have returned. "We can't visit the Iron Cross with you looking like that. There are probably tourists there, and they would be frightened."

I didn't pay any attention to him. I got up, brushed off the dust, and saw that I could walk. Petrus suggested that I do the RAM Breathing Exercise, and he picked up my knapsack. I did the exercise and returned once again to a sense of harmony with the world. In half an hour, I would be at the Iron Cross.

And someday, Foncebadon was going to rise from its ruins. Legion had left a lot of power there.

Command and Obedience

@

Petrus was carrying me as we
arrived at the Iron Cross; my leg wound prevented me from
walking. When he realized the extent of the damage done by
the dog, he decided that I should rest until the wound had
healed enough for us to continue along the Strange Road to
Santiago. Nearby there was a village that provided shelter for
pilgrims who were overtaken by nightfall before crossing the
mountains, and Petrus found us two rooms in the home of
a blacksmith.

My haven had a small veranda, an architectural feature
we hadn't seen previously along the Road. From it, I could
see the range of mountains we would have to cross sooner or
later in order to reach Santiago. I fell into bed and slept
until the following day; although I felt slightly feverish when
I awoke, I also felt better.

Petrus brought some water from the fountain that the
villagers called "the bottomless well," and he bathed my
wounds. In the afternoon, he came to my room with an old
woman who lived nearby. They placed several different types
of herbs on the wounds and lacerations, and the woman

made me drink some bitter tea. Petrus insisted that I lick the wounds until they had completely closed. I can still remember the sweet, metallic flavor of my blood; it nauseated me, but my guide told me that my saliva was a powerful disinfectant.

The fever returned during the second day. Petrus and the old woman again plied me with the tea, and they again put the herbs on my wounds. But the fever, although it was not high, continued. My guide decided to go to a military base nearby to see if he could get some bandages, since there was no place in the entire village where gauze or adhesive tape was available.

Several hours later, Petrus returned with the bandages. He was accompanied by a young medical officer, who insisted on knowing where the animal was that had attacked me.

"From the type of bite you have, the animal was rabid," he told me.

"No, no," I said. "I was just playing with him, and it got out of control. I have known the dog for a long time."

The medical officer was not convinced. He insisted that I take an antirabies vaccine, and I was forced to let him administer at least one dose or else I would have been transferred to the base hospital. Afterward, he again asked where the animal was.

"In Foncebadon," I answered.

"Foncebadon is a city in ruins. There are no dogs there," he said, with an air of having found out the lie.

I began to moan as though I were in pain, and Petrus led the young officer out of the room. But he left everything we would need: clean bandages, adhesive tape, and a styptic compound.

Petrus and the old woman refused to use the compound. They bound the wounds with gauze and herbs instead. This made me happy, because it meant that I would no longer have to lick the places where the dog had bitten me. During the night, they both knelt at my bedside and, with their hands placed on my body, prayed aloud for me. I asked Petrus what he was doing, and he made a vague reference to the divine graces and the Road to Rome. I wanted him to tell me more, but he said nothing else.

Two days later, I had recuperated completely. That morning, I looked out my window and saw some soldiers conducting a search of the houses nearby and of the hills around the village. I asked one of them what was happening.

"There is a rabid dog somewhere around here," he answered.

That afternoon, the blacksmith in whose rooms we were staying came to me and asked that I leave the town as soon as I was able to travel. The story had spread among the townspeople, and they were fearful that I would become rabid and transmit the disease to others. Petrus and the old woman began to argue with the blacksmith, but he was adamant. At one point, he even asserted that he had seen a trickle of foam at the corner of my mouth while I was sleeping.

There was no way to convince him that all of us drool a bit in our sleep. That night, Petrus and the woman prayed incessantly over me, and the next day, limping somewhat, I was once again on the Strange Road to Santiago.

I asked Petrus if he had been worried about my recovery.

"There is an understanding about the Road to Santiago that I have not told you about before," he said. "Once a pilgrimage has begun, the only acceptable excuse for interrupting it is illness. If you had not been able to recover from your wounds and your fever had continued, it would have been an omen, telling us that our pilgrimage had to end there."

But he added, with some pride, that his prayers had been answered. And I was certain that the outcome had been as important for him as it was for me.

The Road was downhill now, and Petrus pointed out that it would be that way for the next two days. We had returned to our usual schedule, with a siesta every afternoon at the time when the sun was fiercest. Because of my bandages, Petrus carried my knapsack. We were no longer in a hurry: the encounter we had been rushing toward was over.

My disposition improved with every hour, and I was quite proud of myself; I had climbed a waterfall and defeated the demon of the Road. All that remained was the most important task: to find my sword. I mentioned this to Petrus.

"Your victory was beautiful, but you failed in the most critical sense," he said, throwing a deluge of cold water over me.

"What do you mean?"

"Knowing the right moment for the encounter. I had to hurry us along, setting a pace that was demanding, and the only thing you could think about was that we were after your sword. What good is a sword if you don't know where you are going to run into your enemy?"

"The sword is the instrument of my power," I answered.

"You are too preoccupied with your power," he said. "The waterfall, the RAM practices, the dialogues with your messenger—they all made you forget that there was your enemy to vanquish. And forget that you had an impending encounter with him. Before your hand can wield the sword, you have to discover where your enemy is and how to deal with him. The sword only strikes a blow, but the hand is already victorious or defeated before the blow is delivered.

"You defeated Legion without your sword. There is a secret in this search, and it is a secret you have not yet learned. If you do not do so, you will never find what you are looking for."

I didn't answer him. Every time I began to feel that I was getting close to my objective, Petrus insisted on reminding me that I was just a simple pilgrim and that there was always something else I needed in order to find what I was looking for. The happiness I had been feeling a few minutes before we began the conversation now disappeared completely.

Once again I was starting out on the Strange Road to Santiago, and I was totally discouraged. Along the same Road that I was walking, millions of souls had passed during the past twelve centuries, going to and returning from Santiago de Compostela. In their case, getting to where they had wanted to go had only been a matter of time. In my case, the traps set by the Tradition were forever placing another obstacle in my path and creating new tests for me.

I told Petrus that I was growing tired, and we sat down in the shade. There were huge wooden crosses along the side of the road. Petrus put the two knapsacks on the ground and spoke again: "Our enemy always represents our weaker side. This may be a fear of physical pain, but it may also be a premature sense of victory or the desire to abandon the fight because we define it as not being worth the effort.

"Our enemy joins the battle only because he knows that he can hurt us—and hurt us in exactly the spot where our pride tells us that we are most invincible. During the fight, we always try to protect our weak spot, so the enemy strikes at the unguarded side—the side in which we have the most confidence. And we wind up defeated because we allow what should never be allowed: we let the enemy choose how the battle will be waged."

Everything Petrus was describing had happened during my fight with the dog. Yet I told him that I could not accept the idea that I had enemies and that I had to do battle with them. I said that when Petrus had spoken of the good fight, I had thought that he had been talking about fighting for achievements in one's life.

"That's right," he said. "But that is not all the good fight is. Going to war is not a sin. It is an act of love. The enemy develops us and sharpens us, as the dog did with you."

"OK, I understand that. But let's get back to what we were talking about before. Why is it that you never seem to be satisfied with what I do? I have the impression that you always think I am going about things the wrong way. And weren't you about to tell me the secret of my sword?"

Petrus said that this was something I should have learned before beginning the pilgrimage. And he went on about the enemy.

"Our enemy is part of agape, there to test our grip, our will, and our handling of the sword. He was placed in our lives—and we in his—with a purpose. And that purpose has to be met. So to flee from the battle is the worst thing that could happen. It is worse than losing the fight, because we can always learn something from defeat; if we flee, all we do is declare that our enemy has won."

I said I was surprised to hear him say that; it amazed me to hear a man who seemed to feel so close to Jesus talk about violence in this way.

"Think about why Jesus needed Judas so," he said. "He had to choose an enemy, or his battle here on earth could not have been glorified."

The wooden crosses along the road testified to how that glory had been achieved: with blood, treason, and desertion. I got up and said I was ready to move on.

As we walked, I asked him what, in a battle situation, was a person's greatest source of strength in trying to defeat the enemy.

"Your present. We defend ourselves best through what we are doing right now, because that is where agape and the will to win, through enthusiasm, are.

"And there's another thing I want to make very clear: the enemy rarely represents evil. He is an everyday presence, and it is he that keeps our sword from rusting in its scabbard."

I remembered that once, when we were building a summer house, my wife had decided suddenly to change the location of one of the rooms. It had been my job to give this disagreeable news to the builder. I had called him, a man of about seventy years of age, and told him what I wanted. He had looked at the plan, thought about it, and come up with an even better solution, using a wall that he had already begun to raise. My wife had loved the idea.

Maybe it was this that Petrus was trying to describe in a more complicated way: that we have to use the thrust of what we are doing right now to defeat the enemy.

I told him the story about the builder.

"Life always teaches us more than the Road to Santiago does," he answered. "But we don't have much faith in what life teaches us."

There were crosses all along this part of the Jacobean route. They were made of such massive, heavy wood that the pilgrim who put them there must have had an almost superhuman strength. A cross had been placed every thirty meters for as far as I could see. I asked Petrus what their significance was.

"An ancient and obsolete instrument of torture," he said.

"But why are they here?"

"They must have been some kind of pledge. How should I know?"

We stopped in front of one of them that had toppled over.

"Maybe the wood rotted," I said.

"It's the same wood as all the others. And none of the others rotted."

"Then it must not have been sunk into the earth firmly enough."

Petrus stopped and looked around. He put his knapsack on the ground and sat down. We had stopped to rest only a few minutes before, so I couldn't understand what he was doing. Instinctively, I looked around, expecting to see the dog.

"You defeated the dog," he said, knowing what I was thinking. "Don't worry about the ghosts of the dead."

"Well, then, why are we stopping?"

Petrus made a gesture that told me to be quiet, and I did not say anything for several minutes. I felt the old fear of the dog and decided to remain standing, hoping Petrus would say something.

"What do you hear?" he asked me.

"Nothing. The silence."

"We are not smart enough to be able to listen to the silence! We are just human beings, and we don't even know how to listen to our own ramblings. You have never asked me how I knew that Legion was about to arrive. Now I will tell you how: by listening. The sound began many days before, when we were still in Astorga. Starting then, I began to move along more quickly, because all the indications were that we were going to meet up with him in Foncebadon. You heard the same sound as I, but you were not listening.

"Everything is contained in sounds—the past, the present, and the future. The person who does not know how to listen will never hear the advice that life offers us all the time. And only the person who listens to the sounds of the moment is able to make the right decisions."

Petrus bade me sit down and forget about the dog. He said that he was going to teach me one of the easiest and most important practices of the Road to Santiago.

And he explained the Listening Exercise to me.

"Do it right now," he said.

I began to perform the exercise. I heard the wind and a woman's voice far in the distance, and at one point I sensed that a branch was being broken. It was not a difficult exercise,

THE LISTENING EXERCISE

Relax. Close your eyes.

Try for several minutes to concentrate on all of the sounds you hear in your surroundings, as if you were hearing an orchestra playing its instruments.

Little by little, try to separate each sound from the others. Concentrate on each one, as if it were the only instrument playing. Try to eliminate the other sounds from your awareness.

When you do this exercise every day, you will begin to hear voices. First, you will think that they are imaginary. Later, you will discover that they are voices of people from your past, present, and future, all of them participating with you in the remembrance of time.

This exercise should be performed only when you already know the voice of your messenger.

Do this exercise for ten minutes at a time.

and I was fascinated by its simplicity. I put my ear to the ground and began to listen to the muted sounds of the earth. After a few moments, I began to separate the sounds from each other: the sound of the leaves rustling, the sound of the voice in the distance, and the noise of the beating of the wings of birds. An animal grunted, but I could not identify what kind of beast it was. The fifteen minutes I spent on the exercise flew by.

"After a while, you will see that this exercise will help you to make the right decision," Petrus said, without asking me what I had heard. "Agape speaks to you through the Blue Sphere Exercise, but it also speaks to you through your sight, your sense of touch, through scents, and your heart, and your hearing. A week from now, at the most, you will begin to hear voices. At first, they will be timid, but before long they are going to begin to tell you things that are important. Be careful, though, with your messenger. He is going to try to confuse you. However, you already know the sound of his voice, so he will no longer be a threat."

Petrus asked if I had heard the joyful call of an enemy, or an invitation offered by a woman, or the secret of my sword.

"I just heard the voice of a woman in the distance," I said. "But it was a farmer's wife calling to her child."

"Well, look at that cross there, and see if you can raise it with your thoughts."

I asked him what such an exercise would mean.

"It means having faith in your thoughts," he responded.

I sat down on the ground in a yoga position. I was certain that after everything I had accomplished with the dog and with the waterfall, I was going to be able to do this, too. I fixated on the cross. I imagined myself leaving my body, grasping the cross, and raising it using my astral body. On the road of the Tradition, I had already performed some of these small "miracles." I had been able to shatter glasses and porcelain statues and to move objects along the surface of a table. It was an easy magic trick, and even though it did not signify any great power, it was useful in winning over nonbelievers. I had never tried it, though, with an object the size and weight of the cross. But if Petrus had commanded that I do so, I felt I would know how to make it happen.

For half an hour I tried everything I could. I used astral displacement and suggestion. I remembered the power my Master had over the force of gravity, and I tried to repeat the words that he always used on such occasions. Nothing happened. I was concentrating completely, but the cross did not budge. I invoked Astrain, and he appeared between the columns of fire. But when I spoke to him about the cross, he said that he detested crosses.

Petrus finally shook me to bring me out of my trance.

"Come on, this is becoming irritating," he said. "Since you can't do it by thinking, put the cross upright with your hands."

"With my hands?"

"Do it!"

I was startled. Suddenly the man in front of me had become nasty, very different from the person who had cared for my wounds. I didn't know what to say or do.

"Do it!" he repeated. "I am ordering you to do it!"

There I was, with my arms and hands wrapped in bandages because of the dog's attack. I had just been through the Listening Exercise, but I couldn't believe what I was hearing from Petrus. Without saying anything, I showed him my bandages. But he continued to look coldly at me, not changing his expression in the least. He expected me to obey him. The guide and friend who had accompanied me all this time, who had taught me the RAM practices and told me the beautiful stories about the Road to Santiago, seemed no longer to be there. In his place I saw a man who regarded me as a slave and had ordered me to do something that was stupid.

"What are you waiting for?" he asked.

I remembered the waterfall experience. I recalled that on that day I had had some doubts about Petrus but that then he had been generous with me. He had demonstrated his love and had kept me from giving up on my sword. I could not understand how the same person who had been so kind could be so harsh now. He suddenly seemed to represent the very thing that the human race was trying to put behind it—the oppression of one person by another.

"Petrus, I . . ."

"Do it, or the Road to Santiago ends right here!"

I was scared again. At that moment, I was more frightened than I had been at the waterfall; I was more fearful of him than of the dog that had terrorized me for so long. I prayed that a signal would come to me from somewhere in our surroundings, that I would see or hear something that would explain his senseless command. But we were engulfed in silence. I either had to obey Petrus or forget about the sword. Once again, I raised my bandaged arms, but he sat down on the ground, waiting for me to carry out his orders.

So I decided to obey him.

I went to the cross and tried to budge it with my foot to test its weight. It hardly moved. Even if my hands had been in good shape, I would have had a very difficult time trying to lift it, and I knew that with my hands bound as they were, the task would be almost impossible. But I was going to comply. I was going to die in the attempt, if that was necessary; I was going to sweat blood, as Jesus had when he had had to carry the same kind of burden. But Petrus was going to perceive the seriousness of my effort, and perhaps that would touch him in some way and he would free me from the test.

The cross had broken at its base, but it was still attached to it. I had no knife with which to cut through the fibers. Forgetting about my pain, I put my arms around the cross and tried to wrench it from the shattered base, without using my hands. The wood abraded the lacerations on my arms, and I cried out in pain. I looked at Petrus, and he was completely impassive. I resolved that I would not cry out again. From that moment on, I would stifle any such demonstration.

I knew that my immediate problem was not to move the cross but to free it from its base. Afterward, I would have to dig a hole and push the cross into it. I found a stone with an edge to it and, ignoring the pain, began to pound at the wooden fibers.

The pain was terrible and grew worse with every blow, and the fibers were parting very slowly. I had to give up that approach right away, before my wounds reopened and the whole effort became impossible. I decided to work at it more slowly so that I could accomplish the task without succumbing to the pain. I took off my shirt, wrapped it around my hand, and went back to the job with this additional protection. The idea was a good one: the first fiber parted, and then the second. The stone was losing its edge, so I looked around for another. Each time I paused, I had the feeling that I would not be able to start again. I gathered several sharp stones and used them, one after the other, so that the pain in the hand I was working with was bearable. Almost all of the fibers had been cut, but the main one still held firm. The pain in my hand was increasing, and abandoning the idea of working slowly, I began to strike at the wood frantically. I knew that I was coming close to the point where the pain would make it impossible to continue. It was just a matter of time until this happened, and I had to make good use of that time. I was sawing and pounding now, and something sticky between my skin and the bandages was making the work even more difficult. It is probably blood, I thought, but then I put it out of my mind. I gritted my teeth, struck harder at the fiber, and it seemed about to break. I was so excited that I stood up and delivered a blow with all my strength to the wood that was causing all my suffering.

With a groan, the cross fell to the side, freed from its base.

My joy lasted only for a few moments. My hand was throbbing violently, and I had only begun the job. I looked over at Petrus and saw that he was sleeping. I stood there for a time, trying to figure out some way of fooling him, of putting the cross upright without his noticing it.

But that was exactly what Petrus wanted: that I raise the cross. And there was no way to deceive him, because the task depended solely on me.

I looked at the ground—the dry, yellow earth. Once again, stones would be my only tools. I could not work anymore with my right hand because it hurt too much, and there was that sticky substance under the bandage that worried me. I carefully unwrapped the shirt from the bandages; blood was staining the gauze—and this was a wound that had almost healed. Petrus was a monster!

I found a different kind of stone, one that was heavier and more resistant. Rolling the shirt around my left hand, I began to beat at the earth, trying to dig a hole at the foot of the cross. My initial progress was good, but it was soon slowed by the hardness and dryness of the ground. I kept digging, but the hole seemed to stay the same depth. I decided that I would not make the hole very wide so that the cross would fit into it without wobbling, but this made it more difficult to remove the dirt from the excavation. My right hand had stopped hurting as much as it had, but the coagulated blood made me nauseated and anxious. I was not used to working with my left hand, and the stone kept slipping from my grip.

I dug forever! Every time the stone beat on the ground, and every time I put my hand into the hole to remove some dirt, I thought of Petrus. I looked over at him, dozing peacefully, and I hated him from the bottom of my heart. Neither the noise nor my hatred appeared to disturb him. "He must have his reasons," I said to myself, but I could not understand the debasement and humiliation he was inflicting on me. I saw his face in the earth I was pounding, and the rage I was feeling helped me to dig the hole deeper. Again, it was just a matter of time: sooner or later I was going to win.

As I thought about this, the rock hit something solid and sprang back. This was my worst fear. After all that work, I had run into a stone that was too big for me to continue.

I stood up, wiping the sweat from my face, and began to think. I didn't have enough strength to move the cross to another place. I couldn't start again from the beginning because my left hand, now that I had stopped, felt dead. This was worse than pain, and it really scared me. I looked at my fingers, and I was able to move them, but instinct told me that I shouldn't punish the hand anymore.

I looked at the hole. It wasn't deep enough to hold the cross erect.

"The wrong answer will indicate the right one." I remembered the Shadows Exercise and what Petrus had said then. It was also then that he had told me that the RAM practices would make sense only if I could apply them in my daily life. Even in a situation as absurd as the present one, the RAM practices should be of some use.

"The wrong answer will indicate the right one." The impossible solution would be to try to drag the cross to a different place; I no longer had the strength to do that. It was also impossible to try digging deeper into the ground.

So if the impossible answer was to go deeper into the earth, the possible answer was to raise the earth. But how?

And suddenly, all of my love for Petrus was restored. He was right. I could raise the earth!

I began to collect all the stones nearby and placed them around the hole, mixing them with the earth I had removed.

With great effort, I lifted the foot of the cross a little and supported it with stones to raise it higher off the ground. In half an hour, the ground was higher, and the hole was deep enough.

Now I just had to get the cross into the hole. It was the last step, and I had to make it work. One of my hands was numb, and the other was giving me a great deal of pain. My arms were wrapped in bandages. But my back was all right; it had just a few scratches. If I could lie down beneath the cross and raise it bit by bit, I would be able to slide it into the hole.

I stretched out on the ground, feeling the dust in my nose and eyes. With the hand that was numb, I raised the cross a fraction and slid underneath it. Carefully, I adjusted my position so that its trunk rested squarely on my back. I felt its weight and knew that it would be heavy to lift but not impossible. I thought about the Seed Exercise, and very slowly I squirmed into a fetal position, balancing the cross on my back. Several times I thought it was going to fall, but I was working slowly; I was able to sense the direction it might take and correct for it by repositioning my body. I finally achieved the position I wanted, with my knees in front of me and the cross balanced. For a moment, the foot of the cross shook on the pile of stones, but it did not fall out of place.

"It's a good thing I don't have to save the universe," I thought, oppressed by the weight of the cross and everything it represented. A profoundly religious feeling took possession of me. I remembered that another person had carried the cross on his shoulders and that his damaged hands had not been able to free themselves from the wood or the pain as mine could. This religious feeling was loaded down with pain, but I forgot about it immediately because the cross began to shake again.

Then, slowly raising myself up, I began a rebirth. I couldn't look behind me, and sound was my only means of orientation. But just a while ago I had learned how to listen to the world, as if Petrus had guessed that I was going to need this kind of knowledge. I felt the weight of the cross and sensed that the stones were accommodating each other. The cross rose bit by bit, as if to help me in this test. It was as if the cross, itself, wanted to return to its position, framing that section of the Road to Santiago.

One final push was all that was needed. If I could get into a seated position, the trunk of the cross would slide down my back into the hole. One or two of the stones had been dislodged, but the cross was now helping me, since its foot remained in place where I had built up the wall. Finally, a pull on my back indicated that the base was free. It was the final moment, just as at the waterfall when I had had to fight my way through the current: the most difficult moment, because it is then that we fear failure and want to give up before it occurs. Once again I sensed how absurd the task was, trying to raise a cross when all I really wanted to do was find my sword. But none of these thoughts was important. With a sudden thrust, I raised my back, and the cross slid into place. At that moment I recognized once again that fate had been directing the work I had done.

I stood there expecting the cross to fall in the other direction, scattering the stones I had placed. Then I thought that maybe my push had not been strong enough and that the cross was going to fall back on top of me. But what I heard was the muffled sound of something hitting against the bottom of the hole.

I turned carefully. The cross was upright, and it was still trembling from the impact. Some stones were rolling down their slope, but the cross was not going to fall. I quickly put the stones back in place and embraced the cross so that it would stop wavering. I felt alive and hot, certain that the cross had been my friend throughout all of my work. I stepped away slowly, improving the placement of the stones with my feet.

I stood there admiring my work for a long time, until my wounds began to hurt. Petrus was still asleep. I went over to him and nudged him with my foot.

He awoke with a start and looked at the cross.

"Very good," was all that he said. "In Ponferrada, we will change the bandages."

The Tradition

𖠿

I would rather have lifted a tree. That cross on my back had me thinking that my search for wisdom was going to be the death of me."

Looking at my surroundings, my words rang a bit hollow. The cross episode was already history, as if it had happened a long time ago and not just the previous day. It had no relation to the black marble bathroom, the warmth of the water in the hot tub, or the crystal goblet of Rioja wine that I was enjoying. I could not see Petrus, who was in his own bedroom in the luxury suite we had rented in a first-class hotel.

"Why the cross?" I insisted.

"It wasn't easy to convince the man at the front desk that you weren't a beggar," he yelled from his room.

He was changing the subject, and I knew from experience that it would do no good to press the matter. I got up and put on trousers, a clean shirt, and fresh bandages. I had removed the old ones very carefully, expecting to find open wounds, but the scabs had only broken away from the skin slightly and allowed some blood to ooze out. A new scab had already formed, and I was feeling restored and happy.

We had dinner at the hotel restaurant. Petrus asked for the specialty of the house—a Valencia paella—which we ate in silence. After dinner, he suggested a walk.

We left the hotel and walked in the direction of the railroad station. He was in his now-habitual laconic state and said nothing throughout our entire stroll. We came to a train yard, filthy and smelling of oil, and he sat down on the steps of a gigantic locomotive.

"Let's stop here," he said.

I didn't want to get oil stains on my pants, so I decided to stand. I asked him if he wouldn't prefer to walk to the main square of Ponferrada.

"The Road to Santiago is about to end," said my guide, "and since our reality is a lot more similar to these railroad cars, stinking of oil, than to the bucolic retreats we have encountered during our journey, it is better that today's conversation happen here."

Petrus told me to take off my sneakers and my shirt. Then he loosened the bandages on my arms, leaving them freer to move. But he left those on my hands as they were.

"Don't worry," he said. "You are not going to need your hands for this, at least not to hold anything."

He was more serious than usual, and his tone of voice surprised me. Something important was about to happen.

Petrus sat down again on the steps of the locomotive and looked at me for a long time. Then he said, "I am not going to say anything about yesterday's episode. You will discover for yourself what it means, and this will happen only if someday you decide to walk the Road to Rome—the Road of the graces and miracles. I want to tell you just one thing: people who consider themselves to be wise are often indecisive when command is called for and rebellious when they are called upon to obey. They are ashamed to give orders and consider it dishonorable to receive them. Don't ever be that way.

"In the room, you said that the path to wisdom leads to sacrifice. That is wrong. Your learning period did not end yesterday: you still have to find your sword and learn its secret. The RAM practices allow us to engage in the good fight and to have a better chance at winning in life. The experience you had yesterday was only one of the tests along the Road—it was part of the preparation for the Road to Rome. It saddens me that you thought that it might have been the death of you."

He really sounded saddened. I realized that throughout all the time we had spent together, I had always expressed doubt regarding what he was teaching me. I was not a strong, humble Castaneda receiving his teachings from Don Juan; I was an arrogant and fractious man in my approach to the simple RAM practices. I wanted to say this to Petrus, but I knew that it was too late.

"Close your eyes," Petrus said. "Do the RAM Breathing Exercise, and try to harmonize yourself with this iron, this machinery, and this smell of oil. This is our world. You should open your eyes only when I have completed teaching you an exercise."

I closed my eyes, concentrated on the RAM breathing, and felt my body begin to relax. I could hear the noises of the city, some dogs barking in the distance, and the sound of voices in argument not far from where we were. Suddenly, I began to hear Petrus's voice singing an Italian song recorded by Pepino Di Capri that had been a hit when I was a teenager. I didn't understand the words, but the melody brought back happy memories and helped me to reach a state of tranquillity.

"Some time ago," he began, when he had stopped singing, "as I was working on a project that I had to deliver to the mayor's office in Milan, I received a message from my Master. Someone had gone all the way to the end of the road of the Tradition and had not received his sword. I was supposed to guide him along the Road to Santiago.

"I was not surprised at this: I had been expecting such a summons at any time, because I had not yet paid my dues. I had to guide a pilgrim along the Milky Way, just as I had once been guided. But I was nervous because it was the first and only time that I would do this, and I did not know how to carry out my mission."

Petrus's words really surprised me. I thought that he had been a guide dozens of times.

"You came here, and I guided you," he continued. "I must confess that in the beginning it was very hard, because you were much more interested in the intellectual implications of the teachings than in the true meaning of the Road—the Road of the common people. After the encounter with Alfonso, we developed a much stronger, more intense relationship, and I began to believe that I would be able to teach you the secret of your sword. But this did not happen, and now you will have to learn it for yourself during the little time you have left."

This conversation was making me nervous, and I was losing my concentration on the RAM Breathing Exercise. Petrus must have noticed, because he began to sing the song again and stopped only when I was once again relaxed.

"If you discover the secret and find your sword, you will also discover the face of RAM, and you will have the power. But that is not all: in order to achieve total wisdom, you will have to walk the other three Roads, including the secret one, and the secret Road will not be revealed to you, even by someone who has walked it. I am telling you this because we are going to see each other only one more time."

My heart stopped, and involuntarily, I opened my eyes. Petrus was glowing with the kind of brilliance I had only seen around my Master.

"Close your eyes!" he barked, and I immediately obeyed. But I was very upset, and I could not concentrate anymore.

My guide started to sing the Italian song again, and only after a while was I able to relax.

"Tomorrow you are going to receive a note telling you where I am. I will be at a group initiation, a ritual of honor in the Tradition. It is a ritual in honor of all of the men and women who, down through the centuries, have helped to keep alive the flame of wisdom, of the good fight, and of agape. You will not be able to speak to me. The place where we will meet is secret. It is bathed in the blood of all those who have walked the road of the Tradition and who, even with their swords sharpened, were unable to brighten the darkness. But their sacrifice was not in vain, and the proof that it was not is that, centuries later, those who have walked different roads will be there to pay them tribute. This is important, and you should never forget it: even if you become a Master, you have to realize that your road is only one of many that lead to God. Jesus once said, 'In my Father's house, there are many mansions.'"

Petrus repeated that after tomorrow, I would not see him again.

"On some future day, you will receive a message from me, asking you to lead someone along the Road to Santiago, just as I have led you. Then you will be able to experience the great secret of the journey—a secret that I am going to reveal to you now, but only through words. It is a secret that has to be experienced to be understood."

There was a prolonged silence. I began to think that he had changed his mind or that he had left the train yard. I felt an enormous desire to open my eyes to see what was happening, but I forced myself to concentrate on the RAM breathing.

"The secret is the following," Petrus said. "You can learn only through teaching. We have been together here on the

Road to Santiago, but while you were learning the practices, I learned the meaning of them. In teaching you, I truly learned. By taking on the role of guide, I was able to find my own true path.

"If you succeed in finding your sword, you will have to teach the Road to someone else. And only when that happens—when you accept your role as a Master—will you learn all the answers you have in your heart. Each of us knows the answers, even before someone tells us what they are. Life teaches us lessons every minute, and the secret is to accept that only in our daily lives can we show ourselves to be as wise as Solomon and as powerful as Alexander the Great. But we become aware of this only when we are forced to teach others and to participate in adventures as extravagant as this one has been."

I was hearing the most unexpected farewell in my life. The person with whom I had had the most intense bond was saying good-bye right there in midjourney—in an oily-smelling train yard, with me forced to keep my eyes closed.

"I don't like saying good-bye," Petrus continued. "I am Italian, and I am very emotional. But according to the law of the Tradition, you must find your sword alone. This is the only way that you will believe in your own power. I have passed on to you everything that I have to give. The only thing left is the Dance Exercise, which I am going to teach you now; you should perform it tomorrow at the ritual."

He was silent for a while, and then he spoke:

"May that which is glorified be glorified in the Lord. You may open your eyes."

Petrus was still sitting on the locomotive. I did not want to say anything, because I am Brazilian and also emotional. The mercury lamp providing us with light began to flutter, and a train whistled in the distance, announcing its next stop.

It was then that Petrus taught me the Dance Exercise.

THE DANCE EXERCISE

Relax. Close your eyes.

Recall the first songs you heard as a child. Begin to sing them in your thoughts. Little by little, let a certain part of your body—your feet, your stomach, your hands, your head, and so on—but only one part, begin to dance to the melody you are singing.

After five minutes, stop singing, and listen to the sounds all around you. Compose an internal melody based on them, and dance to it with your whole body. Don't think about anything in particular, but try to memorize the images that spontaneously appear.

The dance offers an almost-perfect means of communication with the Infinite Intelligence.

This exercise should last fifteen minutes.

"One more thing," he said, looking deeply into my eyes. "When I completed my pilgrimage, I painted a beautiful, immense picture that depicted everything that had happened to me here. This is the Road of the common people, and you can do the same thing, if you like. If you don't know how to paint, write something, or create a ballet. Then, regardless of where they are, people will be able to walk the Jacobean route, the Milky Way, the Strange Road to Santiago."

The train that had sounded its whistle began to enter the station. Petrus waved to me and disappeared between the parked railroad cars. I stood there amid the noise of brakes screeching on steel, trying to decipher the mysterious Milky Way over my head, those stars that had guided me here and that had silently watched over the loneliness and destiny of all human beings.

Next day, there was just a note left in my room: 7:00 P.M.—CASTLE OF THE TEMPLARS.

I spent the rest of that afternoon walking around the streets aimlessly. I crossed and recrossed the small city of Ponferrada, looking from a distance at the castle on the hill where I had been bidden to appear. The Templars had always stirred my imagination, and the castle in Ponferrada was not the only mark made on the Jacobean route by their order. The order had been created by nine knights who had decided not to return from the Crusades. Within a short time, their power had spread throughout Europe, and they had caused a revolution in the values at the beginning of this millennium. While most of the nobility of the time was concerned only with enriching itself through the labor of the serfs, the Knights Templar dedicated their lives, their fortunes, and their swords to one cause only: the protection of the pilgrims that walked the Road to Jerusalem. In the behavior of the Knights, the pilgrims found a model for their own search for wisdom.

In 1118, when Hugh de Payens and eight other knights held a meeting in the courtyard of an old, abandoned castle, they took a vow of love for all humanity. Two centuries later, there were more than five thousand benefices spread throughout the known world; they reconciled two activities that until then had appeared to be incompatible: the military life and the religious one. Donations from the members and from grateful pilgrims allowed the Order of the Knights Templars to accumulate incalculable wealth, which was used more than once to ransom important Christians who had been kidnapped by the Muslims. The honesty of the Knights was such that kings and nobles entrusted their valuables to the Templars and traveled only with a document that attested to the existence of their wealth. This document could be redeemed at any castle of the Order of the Templars for an equivalent sum, giving rise to the letter of credit that is used today.

Their spiritual devotion, in turn, had allowed the Knights Templars to understand the great truth that Petrus had quoted the night before: that the house of the Lord has many mansions. They sought to put an end to religious conflict and to unite the main monotheistic religions of the time: Christian, Jewish, and Islamic. Their chapels were built with the rounded cupola of the Judaic temples of Solomon, the octagonal walls of the Arab mosques, and the naves that were typical of Christian churches.

But as with everything that happens before its time, the Templars came to be viewed with suspicion. The great kings sought to hold economic power, and religious liberalism was regarded as a threat to the Church. On Friday, October 13, 1307, the Vatican and the major European states unleashed one of the most massive police operations of the Middle Ages: during the night, the main leaders of the Templars were seized in their castles and thrown in prison. They were accused of practicing secret ceremonies, including the worship of the devil, of blasphemy against Jesus Christ, of orgiastic rituals, and of engaging in sodomy with their apprentices. Following a violent sequence of torture, renunciation, and treason, the Order of the Templars was erased from the map of medieval history. Their treasures were confiscated, and their members scattered throughout the world. The last master of the Order, Jacques de Molay, was burned at the stake in the center of Paris, along with a fellow Knight. His last request was that he be allowed "to die looking at the towers of the Cathedral of Notre Dame."

Spain, which was struggling to recapture the Iberian peninsula, welcomed the Knights fleeing from other parts of Europe, and the Spanish kings sought their help in the battles against the Moors. These Knights were absorbed into the Spanish orders, one of which was the Order of San Tiago of the Sword, responsible for protection along the Road.

I was thinking about this history when, exactly at seven in the evening, I passed through the main gate of the old Castle of the Templars of Ponferrada, where I was scheduled for an encounter with the Tradition.

There was no one there. I waited for half an hour and then began to fear the worst: that the ritual must have been at 7:00 A.M. But just as I was deciding to leave, two boys appeared, carrying the flag of Holland and with the scallop shell—the symbol of the Road to Santiago—sewn to their clothing. They came up to me, and we exchanged some words, concluding that we were there for the same purpose. I was relieved that the note had not been wrong.

Every fifteen minutes someone else arrived. There were an Australian, five Spaniards, and another man from Holland. Other than a few questions about the schedule—about which everyone was confused—we did not talk at all. We all sat together in the same part of the castle—a ruined atrium that had served as a storeroom for food in ancient times—and we decided to wait until something happened, even if we had to wait another day and night.

The waiting went on, and we fell to talking about the reasons we were there. It was then that I learned that the Road to Santiago is used by a number of different orders, most of them part of the Tradition. The people who were there had already been through many tests and initiations of the kind that I had gone through long ago in Brazil. Only the Australian and I were expecting to be conferred the highest degree of the first Road. Even without knowing the details, I could see that the process the Australian had gone through was completely different from the RAM practices.

At about 8:45, as we were beginning to talk about our personal lives, a gong rang. We followed the sound to the ancient chapel of the castle.

There we found an impressive scene. The chapel—or what remained of it, since most of it was in ruins—was illuminated only by torches. Where there had once been an altar could be seen seven figures garbed in the secular costumes of the Templars: a hood and steel helmet, a coat of mail, a sword, and a shield. I gasped: it was a scene from the distant past. All that made the situation seem real were our own suits and jeans and our shirts with the scallop shell emblem.

Even with the faint illumination provided by the torches, I could see that one of the Knights was Petrus.

"Approach your Masters," said the Knight who appeared to be the oldest. "Look into the eyes of your Master. Take off your clothes and receive your vestments."

I went to Petrus and looked deeply into his eyes. He was in a kind of trance and seemed not to recognize me. But I could see in his eyes a certain sadness, the same sadness that his voice had conveyed on the previous night. I took all of my clothes off, and Petrus handed me a perfumed black tunic that fell loosely around my body. I surmised that one of the

Masters had more than one disciple, but I could not see which he was because of the requirement that I keep my eyes fixed on those of Petrus.

The High Priest directed us to the center of the chapel, and two Knights began to trace a circle' around us as they chanted: "Trinitas, Sother, Messias, Emmanuel, Sabahot, Adonai, Athanatos, Jesus . . ."[1]

The circle was being drawn to provide the protection needed for those within it. I noticed that four of us had white tunics, signifying vows of total chastity.

"Amides, Throdonias, Anitor!" intoned the High Priest. "By the grace of the angels, Lord, I provide the vestment of salvation; I pray that everything I desire be transformed into reality, through thee, O my sacred Adonai, whose kingdom is forever. Amen!"

The High Priest placed over his coat of mail the white mantle with the Templar's Cross outlined in red in the center. The other Knights did the same.

It was exactly nine o'clock, the hour of Mercury, the messenger. And there I was, once again within the circle of the Tradition. There was an incense of mint, basil, and benjamin burning in the chapel, and the grand invocation of the Knights began:

"O great and glorious King, who rules through the power of the Supreme God, EL, over all higher and lower spirits, but especially over the Infernal Order of the Dominion of the East, I invoke you . . . so that I may realize my wish,

---

[1]Since this is an extremely long ritual and can be understood only by those who know the road of the Tradition, I have opted to summarize the incantations used. But this does not change the narrative at all, since this ritual was performed only to establish a reunion with and respect for the ancients. The important element of this part of the Road to Santiago—the Dance Exercise—is described here in its entirety.

whatever that may be, so long as it is proper to your labors, through the power of our God, EL, who created and provided all things celestial, of the air, of the earth, and of the infernal realm."

A profound silence followed, and even without being able to see him, we could sense the presence of the being who had been the object of the invocation. This was the consecration of the ritual, a propitious sign that we should continue with our magical activities. I had already participated in hundreds of similar ceremonies, at some of which the results up to this point had been much more surprising. But the Castle of the Templars must have stimulated my imagination a little, because I thought I saw, hovering in the corner of the chapel, a kind of shining bird that I had never seen before.

The High Priest sprinkled water over us without stepping into the circle. Then, with the sacred ink, he wrote in the earth the seventy-two names by which God is known within the Tradition.

All of us—pilgrims and Knights—began to recite the sacred names. The flames of the torches crackled, a sign that the spirit that had been invoked had surrendered.

The moment for the dance had arrived. I knew how to participate because Petrus had taught me on the previous day; it was a different dance from the one I was used to performing at this stage during similar rituals.

No rule was stated, but all of us already knew what it was: no initiate could step outside the protective circle, since we lacked the protection that the Knights had with their suits of mail. I visualized the size of the circle and did exactly as Petrus had taught me.

I thought back to my infancy. A voice, the far-off voice of a woman within me, began to sing a simple melody. I knelt and compressed myself into the seed position and felt that my breast—only my breast—was beginning to dance. I felt at ease, able to enter completely into the ritual of the Tradition. The music within me began to change; my movements became more pronounced, and I entered into a powerful state of ecstasy. Everything around me was darkened, and my body, surrounded by that darkness, felt weightless. I saw myself walking through the flowered fields of Aghata, where I met my grandmother and an uncle who had been important to me when I was a child. I felt the vibration of time in its grid of quadrants, where all roads are joined and mixed, becoming identical despite their being so different from each other. At one point, I saw the Australian flash by me: his body was suffused in a red glow.

The image that followed was of a chalice and paten, and this image lasted for a long time, as if it had a special importance for me. I tried to understand its significance, but nothing came to me, despite my conviction that it had something to do with my sword. Then, after the chalice and paten had vanished, I saw the face of RAM coming toward me out of the darkness. But when the face came closer, it was only the face of N., the spirit that had been invoked, who was well known to me. We did not establish any special kind of communication, and his face dissolved into the darkness that was fluctuating around me.

I don't know how long we continued to dance. But suddenly I heard a voice:

"YAHWEH, TETRAGRAMMATON . . ." and I didn't want to emerge from my trance, but the voice insisted:

"YAHWEH, TETRAGRAMMATON . . ." and I recognized the voice of the High Priest, calling upon everyone to come out of the trance. It irritated me. The Tradition was where I was rooted, and I did not want to come back. But the Master demanded it:

I couldn't maintain the trance. Resentfully, I returned to earth. I was once again within the magic circle there in the ancestral ambiance of the Castle of the Templars.

We pilgrims looked at each other. The sudden interruption seemed to have displeased everyone. I felt a strong urge to tell the Australian that I had seen him in my trance. But when I looked over at him, I saw that it wasn't necessary: he had seen me, too.

The Knights came to us and surrounded us. They began to beat upon their shields with their hands, making a noise that was deafening. Then the High Priest spoke:

"O Spirit N., because thou so diligently responded to my requests, with all due solemnity I allow thee to depart, without injury to man or beast. Go, I command thee, and be ready and anxious to return whenever thou art duly exorcised and conjured by the sacred rites of the Tradition. I conjure thee to go, peacefully and quietly, and may God's peace continue ever to be with thee and me. Amen."

The circle was erased, and we knelt with our heads bowed. A Knight said seven Paternosters and seven Ave Marias with us. The High Priest added seven repetitions of the Apostles' Creed, stating that Our Lady of Medjugorje—whose visitations had been noted in Yugoslavia ever since 1982—had indicated that he should do this. And then we began another of the Christian rituals.

"Andrew, rise and come before me," said the High Priest. The Australian approached the altar, where the seven Knights were standing.

One of the Knights—the one who must have been his guide—spoke:

"Brother, dost thou demand the company of the House?"

"Yes," answered the Australian. And then I understood which of the Christian rituals we were witnessing: the initiation of a Templar.

"Dost thou understand the great severities of the House and its charitable orders?"

"I am ready to support all of them, in God's name, and I desire to be a servant and slave of the House forever, through all the days of my life," answered the Australian.

There followed a series of ritual questions, some of which made no sense in today's world; others were concerned with profound devotion and love. Andrew, with his head bowed, responded to all of them.

"Distinguished brother, thou art asking a great thing of me. But thou art seeing only the outer layer of our religion— the beautiful horses and the elegant vestments," said his guide. "But thou knowest not the hard demands made here within: it will be difficult for thee, who art master of thyself, to serve others; rarely wilt thou be able to do as thou wishest. If thou desirest that thou be here, thou wilt be sent beyond the sea, and if thou desirest that thou be in Acre, thou wilt be sent to Tripoli, or Antioch, or Armenia. And when thou desirest sleep, thou wilt be told to stand guard, and when thou wantest to stand guard, thou wilt be told to sleep in thy bed."

"I desire to enter the House," answered the Australian. It felt as if all of the Templars who had ever lived in the castle were happily attending the initiation ceremony; the torches were crackling in earnest.

Several admonishments followed, and the Australian answered them all by saying that he wanted to enter the House. Finally, his guide turned to the High Priest and repeated all of the answers the Australian had made. The High Priest solemnly asked once more if he was ready to accept all of the rules of the House.

"Yes, Master, God willing. I come before God, before thee, and before the brothers, and I implore and solicit thee, before God and Our Lady, to take me into thy company and into the favors of the House, spiritually and temporally, as one who desires to be servant and slave of the House from now on, for all the days of his life."

"I bid you enter, by God's love," said the High Priest.

With that, all of the Knights unsheathed their swords and pointed them toward heaven. Then they lowered the blades and made of them a crown of steel around Andrew's head. The flames created a golden reflection on the blades, consecrating the moment.

Solemnly his Master came to him. And he gave him his sword.

Someone began to toll a bell, and its notes echoed off the walls of the ancient castle, infinitely repeating themselves. We all bowed our heads, and the Knights disappeared from view. When we looked up, we were only ten; the Australian had left to join the Knights in the ritual banquet.

We changed back into our street clothes and said our good-byes without any further formalities. The dance must have lasted for a long time, because the day was brightening. An immense loneliness invaded my soul.

I was envious of the Australian, who had recovered his sword and had reached the end of his quest. Now I was alone, with no one to guide me; the Tradition—in a distant country in South America—had expelled me without showing me the road back. And I had to continue to walk the Strange Road to Santiago, which was now coming to an end, without knowing the secret of my sword or how to find it.

The bell continued to toll. As I left the castle, with dawn breaking, I noticed that it was the bell of a nearby church, calling the faithful to the first mass of the day. The people of the city were awakening to their work and their unpaid bills, their love affairs and their dreams. But they didn't know that, on the previous night, an ancestral rite had once again taken place, that what had been thought of as dead and gone for centuries had once again been celebrated, and that it continued to demonstrate its awesome power.

El Cebrero

6

Are you a pilgrim?" asked the little girl. She was the only person in sight on that blazing afternoon in Villafranca del Bierzo.

I looked at her but didn't answer. She was about eight and poorly dressed. She had run to the fountain where I had sat down to rest.

My only concern now was to get to Santiago de Compostela as quickly as possible and put an end to this crazy adventure. I had not been able to forget the sadness in Petrus's voice at the train yard nor the way he had looked at me from a distance when I had met his gaze during the ritual of the Tradition. It was as if all of the effort he had made in helping me had led to nothing. When the Australian had been called to the altar, I was sure that Petrus would have preferred that it had been I who had been called. My sword might very well be hidden in that castle, the repository of legends and ancient wisdom. It was a place that fit perfectly with all of my deductions: deserted, visited only by a few pilgrims who respected the relics of the Order of the Templars, and located on sacred ground.

But only the Australian had been called to the altar. And Petrus must have felt humiliated in the presence of the others because, as a guide, he had not been capable of leading me to my sword.

Besides this, the ritual of the Tradition had aroused in me again a bit of my fascination with occult wisdom, most of which I had forgotten about as I made my way along the Strange Road to Santiago, the Road of the common people. The invocations, the absolute control over the material, the communication with other worlds—all of that was much more interesting to me than the RAM practices. But perhaps the practices had a more objective application in my life; there was no doubt that I had changed a lot since I had begun to walk the Strange Road to Santiago. Thanks to Petrus's help, I had learned that I could pass through waterfalls, win out over enemies, and converse with my messenger about practical matters. I had seen the face of my death and the blue sphere of the love that consumes and floods the entire world. I was ready to fight the good fight and turn my life into a series of triumphs.

Yet a hidden part of me was still nostalgic for the magic circles, the transcendental formulas, the incense, and the sacred ink. The ceremony that Petrus had called an "homage to the ancients" had been for me an intense and healthful encounter with old, forgotten lessons. And the possibility that I might never again have access to that world discouraged me from wanting to go on.

When I had returned to my hotel after the ritual of the Tradition, there in my box, along with my key, was a copy of *The Pilgrim's Guide*. This was a book that Petrus had utilized for orientation when the yellow markers were hard to find; it had helped us to calculate the distances between cities. I left Ponferrada that same morning, without having slept, and went out on the Road. By that afternoon, I had discovered that the map was not drawn to scale, and that I had to spend a night out in the open, in a cave in the cliffs.

There, as I meditated on everything that had happened to me since my meeting with Mme Lourdes, I thought about the relentless effort Petrus had made to help me understand that contrary to what we had always been taught, results *were* what counted. One's efforts are salutary and indispensable, but without results, they amount to nothing. And now the only result that I demanded of myself, the only reward for everything I had been through, was to find my sword. That had not happened yet, and Santiago was only a few days away.

"If you are a pilgrim, I can take you to the Gates of Forgiveness," insisted the girl at the fountain in Villafranca del Bierzo. "Whoever passes through those gates need not go all the way to Santiago."

I held out some pesetas to her so that she would go away and leave me alone. But instead she began to splash the water in the fountain, wetting my knapsack and my shorts.

"Come on, come on," she said again. At that moment, I was thinking about one of Petrus's repeated quotations: "He that ploweth should plow in hope. He that thresheth in hope should be partaker of his hope." It was from one of the letters of the apostle Paul.

. I had to persevere for a little longer, to continue searching until the end, without being fearful of defeat, to keep alive the hope of finding my sword and understanding its secret.

And—who knows?—was this little girl trying to tell me something that I didn't want to understand? If the Gates of Forgiveness, which were part of a church, had the same spiritual effect as arriving at Santiago, why couldn't my sword be there?

"Let's go," I said to the child. I looked at the mountain that I had just descended; I was going to have to climb part of it again. I had passed by the Gates of Forgiveness with no desire to go to them, since my only goal was to get to Santiago. Now, here was a little girl, the only human being present there on that hot afternoon, insisting that I go back and see something I had decided to ignore. After all, why hadn't that little girl gone away after I had given her some money? Could it be that, in my discouragement and haste, I had walked right past my objective without recognizing it?

Petrus had always said that I liked to fantasize too much about things. But perhaps he was wrong.

As I walked along with the girl, I was remembering the story of the Gates of Forgiveness. They represented a kind of "arrangement" that the Church had made for pilgrims who fell sick. From that point on, the Road became once again difficult and mountainous all the way to Compostela, so during the twelfth century, one of the popes had said that whoever was unable to go further had only to pass through the Gates of Forgiveness to receive the same indulgences as the pilgrims who made it to the end of the Road. With one magic gesture, that pope had resolved the problem posed by the mountains and had inspired an increased number of pilgrimages.

We climbed, following the same route I had traveled earlier in the day: twisting roads, slippery and steep. The girl led, moving along very quickly, and many times I had to ask that she go more slowly. She would do so for a while and then, losing her sense of pace, would begin to run again. Half an hour later, and after much grumbling on my part, we reached the Gates of Forgiveness.

"I have the key to the church," she said. "I will go in and open the gates so you can pass through them."

She went in through the main entrance, and I waited outside. It was a small church, and the gates opened to the north. The door frame was decorated with scallop shells and scenes from the life of San Tiago. As I heard the sound of the key in the lock, an immense German shepherd, appearing out of nowhere, came up to me and stood between the portal and me.

I was immediately prepared for a fight. "Not again," I thought. "Is this story never going to end? Nothing but more and more tests, battles, and humiliations—and still no clue about my sword."

At that moment, though, the Gates of Forgiveness swung open, and the girl appeared. When she saw that the dog was watching me—and that my eyes were already fixed on his—she said some affectionate words to him, and the dog relaxed. Wagging his tail, he followed her toward the back of the church.

Maybe Petrus was right. Maybe I did like to fantasize about things. A simple German shepherd had been transformed in my mind into a threatening supernatural being. That was a bad sign—a sign of the fatigue that leads to defeat.

But there was still hope. The girl signaled to me to enter. With my heart full of expectation, I passed through the Gates of Forgiveness, thereby receiving the same indulgences as the pilgrims who went all the way to Santiago.

My gaze swept over the empty, undecorated church, seeking the only thing I cared about.

"At the top of all the columns you can see shells. The shell is the symbol of the Road," began the girl. "This is Santa Agueda of . . ."

Before long, I could see that it had been useless to come all the way back to this church.

"And this is San Tiago Matamoros, brandishing his sword. You can see dead Moors under his horse's hooves. This statue was made in . . ."

San Tiago's sword was there but not mine. I offered a few more pesetas to the girl, but she would not accept them.

A bit offended, she ended her explanations about the church and asked me to leave.

Once again I walked down the mountain and resumed my pilgrimage toward Compostela. As I passed through Villafranca del Bierzo for the second time, a man approached me. He said that his name was Angel and asked if I would be interested in seeing the Church of Saint Joseph the Carpenter. The man's name gave me hope, but I had just been disappointed, and I was beginning to see that Petrus was an expert observer of behavior. People do have a tendency to fantasize about things that do not even exist, while they fail to learn the lessons that are before their very eyes.

But perhaps just to confirm this tendency one more time, I allowed myself to be led by Angel to this other church. It was closed, and he did not have a key. He pointed to the framework of the entrance with its carving of Saint Joseph, his carpentry tools close alongside him. I nodded, thanked him, and offered him some pesetas. He refused them and left me there in the middle of the street—but not before saying, "We are proud of our city. It is not for money that we do this."

I returned to the Road and in fifteen minutes had left Villafranca del Bierzo behind—Villafranca del Bierzo, with its doors, its streets, and its mysterious guides who asked nothing in exchange for their services.

I walked for some time through mountainous terrain; my progress was slow and demanding. As I started out, I thought only about my previous worries—solitude, shame at having disappointed Petrus, my sword and its secret. But soon the images of the little girl and of Angel began insistently to come to mind. While I had been focusing only on what I would gain, they had done the best for me that they could. And they had asked for nothing in return. A vague idea began to surface from deep inside me. It was some sort of link among all the things I was thinking about. Petrus had always insisted that the expectation of reward was absolutely necessary to the achievement of victory. Yet every time that I forgot about the rest of the world and began to think only about my sword, he forced me, through his painful lessons, to return to reality. This was a sequence that had occurred repeatedly during our time together on the Road.

There was some reason for this, and it was somehow connected with the secret of my sword. What was hiding there inside me began to coalesce and come to light. I still was not sure what it was that I was thinking, but something told me that I was looking in the right direction.

I appreciated having run into the little girl and Angel; they had shown something of the love that consumes in the way they spoke about their churches. They had caused me to go over the same ground twice, and because of this, I had forgotten my fascination with the ritual of the Tradition and had returned to the fields of Spain.

I remembered a day long ago when Petrus had told me that we had walked several times over the same part of the Road in the Pyrenees. I remembered that day with nostalgia. It had been a good beginning, and who knew but what this repetition of that event was not an omen of a positive outcome.

That night I arrived at a village and asked for a room at the home of an old lady. She charged me a pittance for my bed and food. We chatted a bit, and she talked about her faith in Jesus of the Sacred Heart and her worries about the olive crop in that drought year. I drank some wine, had some soup, and went to bed early.

I was feeling better about things, mainly because of the concept that was developing in my mind and the fact that it felt ready for expression. I prayed, did some of Petrus's exercises, and decided to invoke Astrain.

I needed to talk to him about what had happened during the fight with the dog. That day he had almost caused me to lose, and then, after his refusal in the episode of the cross, I had decided to do away with him forever. On the other hand, if I had not recognized his voice during the fight, I would have given in to the temptations that had appeared.

"You did everything possible to help Legion win," I said.

"I do not fight against my brothers," Astrain answered. It was the response I had expected. I had already predicted that he would say this, and it didn't make sense to get irritated with the messenger for being himself. I had to seek out in him the ally who had helped me at times like this, for that was his only function. I put my rancor aside and began to tell him animatedly about the Road, about Petrus, and about the secret of the sword, which I felt was beginning to formulate itself in my mind. He had nothing important to say—only that these secrets were not available to him. But at least I had someone to open up with after having spent the entire afternoon in silence. We had been talking for hours when the old lady rapped on my door to tell me that I was talking in my sleep.

I awoke feeling more optimistic and took to the Road early. According to my calculations, that afternoon I would reach Galicia, the region where Santiago de Compostela was located. It was all uphill, and I had to exert myself for almost four hours to keep to the pace I had set for myself. Every time I reached the crest of a hill I hoped that it would mark the point of descent. But this never seemed to happen, and I had to give up any hope of moving along more rapidly. In the distance I could see mountains that were even higher, and I realized that sooner or later I was going to have to cross them. My physical exertions, meanwhile, had made it impossible to think much, and I began to feel more friendly toward myself.

"Come on now, after all, how can you take seriously anyone who leaves everything behind to look for a sword?"

I asked myself. What would it really mean to my life if I couldn't find it? I had learned the RAM practices, I had gotten to know my messenger, fought with the dog, and seen my death, I told myself, trying to convince myself that the Road to Santiago was what was important to me. The sword was only an outcome. I would like to find it, but I would like even more to know what to do with it. Because I would have to use it in some practical way, just as I used the exercises Petrus had taught me.

I stopped short. The thought that up until then had been only nascent exploded into clarity. Everything became clear, and a tide of agape washed over me. I wished with all my heart that Petrus were there so that I could tell him what he had been waiting to hear from me. It was the only thing that he had really wanted me to understand, the crowning accomplishment of all the hours he had devoted to teaching me as we walked the Strange Road to Santiago: it was the secret of my sword!

And the secret of my sword, like the secret of any conquest we make in our lives, was the simplest thing in the world: it was what I should do with the sword.

I had never thought in these terms. Throughout our time on the Strange Road to Santiago, the only thing I had wanted to know was where it was hidden. I had never asked myself why I wanted to find it or what I needed it for. All of my efforts had been bent on reward; I had not understood that when we want something, we have to have a clear purpose in mind for the thing that we want. The only reason for seeking a reward is to know what to do with that reward. And this was the secret of my sword.

Petrus needed to know that I had learned this, but I was sure I would never see him again. He had waited so long for this, and he would never know that it had happened.

So I knelt there, took some paper from my notebook, and wrote down what I intended to do with my sword. I folded the sheet carefully and placed it under a stone—one that reminded me of him and his friendship. Time would eventually destroy the paper, but symbolically, I was delivering it to Petrus.

Now he knew that I was going to succeed with my sword. My mission with Petrus had been accomplished.

I climbed the mountain, and the agape flowing through me intensified the colors in the surroundings. Now that I had discovered the secret, I had to find what I was looking for. A faith, an unshakable certainty, took control of my being. I began to sing the Italian song that Petrus had remembered in the train yard. I didn't know the words, so I made them up. There was no one in sight, and I was passing through some deep woods, so the isolation made me sing even louder. Shortly I saw that the words I had used made a kind of absurd sense. They were a way of communicating with the world that only I knew, since now it was the world that was teaching me.

I had experimented with this in a different way during my first encounter with Legion. That day, the gift of tongues had manifested itself in me. I had been the servant of the Spirit, which had used me to save a woman and to create an enemy, and had taught me the cruel version of the good fight. Now everything was different: I was my own Master, and I was learning to communicate with the universe.

I began to talk to everything along the Road: tree trunks, puddles, fallen leaves, and beautiful vines. It was an exercise of the common people, learned by children and forgotten by adults. And I received a mysterious response from those things, as if they understood what I was saying; they, in turn, flooded me with the love that consumes. I went into a kind of trance that frightened me, but I wanted to continue the game until I tired of it.

Petrus was right again: by teaching myself, I had transformed myself into a Master.

214

It was time for lunch, but I didn't stop to eat. When I passed through the small villages along the Road, I spoke more softly and smiled to myself, and if by chance someone noticed me, they would have concluded that the pilgrims arriving nowadays at the Cathedral of Santiago were crazy. But this didn't matter to me, because I was celebrating the life all around me and because I knew what I had to do with my sword when I found it.

For the rest of the afternoon, I walked along in a trance, aware of where it was that I wanted to go but more aware of my surroundings and the fact that they had returned agape to me. Heavy clouds began to gather in the sky for the first time in my journey, and I hoped it would rain. After such a long period of hiking and of drought, the rain would be a new, exciting experience. At three in the afternoon, I crossed into Galicia, and I could see on the map that there was one more mountain to climb in order to complete that leg of the pilgrimage. I was determined to climb it and then to sleep in the first town on the other side: Tricastela, where a great king—Alfonso IX—had dreamed of creating an immense city but which, many centuries later, was still a tiny country village.

Still singing and speaking the language I had invented for communicating with the things around me, I began to climb the only remaining mountain: El Cebrero. Its name went back to ancient Roman settlements in the region and was said to mean "February," when something important had presumably happened. In ancient times, this was considered to be the most difficult part of the Jacobean route, but today things have changed. Although the angle of ascent is steeper than in the other mountains, a large television antenna on a neighboring mountain serves as a reference point for pilgrims and prevents their wandering from the Road, a common and fatal event in the past.

The clouds began to lower, and I saw that I would shortly be entering fog. To get to Tricastela, I had to follow the yellow markers carefully; the television antenna was already hidden in the mist. If I got lost, I would wind up sleeping outdoors, and on that day, with the threat of rain, the experience would be quite disagreeable. It is one thing to feel raindrops falling on your face, enjoying the freedom of the life of the Road, and then find a place nearby where you can have a glass of wine and sleep in a bed in preparation for the next day's march. It is quite another to have the raindrops cause a night of insomnia as you try to sleep in the mud, with your wet bandages providing fertile ground for a knee infection.

I had to decide quickly. Either I went forward through the fog—there was still enough light to do so—or I returned to sleep in the small village I had passed through a few hours ago, leaving the crossing of El Cebrero for the next day.

As I realized that I had to make a quick decision, I noticed that something strange was happening. My certainty that I had discovered the secret of my sword was somehow pushing me to go forward into the fog that would shortly engulf me. This feeling was quite different from the one that had made me follow the little girl to the Gates of Forgiveness and made me go with the man to the Church of Saint Joseph the Carpenter.

I remembered that, on the few occasions when I had agreed to put a magic curse on someone in Brazil, I had compared this mystical experience with another very common experience: that of learning to ride a bicycle. You begin by mounting the bicycle, pushing on the pedals, and falling. You try and you fall, try and fall, and you cannot seem to learn how to balance yourself. Suddenly, though, you achieve perfect equilibrium, and you establish complete mastery over the vehicle. It is not a cumulative experience but a kind of "miracle" that manifests itself only when you allow the bicycle "to ride you." That is, you accept the disequilibrium of the two wheels and, as you go along, begin to convert the initial force toward falling into a greater force on the pedal.

At that moment in my ascent of El Cebrero, at four in the afternoon, I saw that the same miracle had occurred. After so much time spent walking the Road to Santiago, the Road to Santiago began to "walk me." I followed what everyone calls one's intuition. And because of the love that consumes that I had experienced all that day, and because my sword's secret had been discovered, and because at moments of crisis a person always makes the right decision, I went forward with no hesitation into the fog.

"This fog has to stop," I thought, as I struggled to see the yellow markers on the stones and trees along the Road. By now the visibility had been very poor for almost an hour, but I continued to sing as an antidote to my fear, while I hoped that something extraordinary would happen. Surrounded by the fog, alone in those unreal surroundings, I began to look at the Road to Santiago as if it were a film; this was the moment when the hero does things that no one else in the film would dare to do, while the audience is thinking that such things only happen in the movies. But there I was, living through a real situation. The forest was growing quieter and quieter, and the fog began to dissipate. I seemed to be reaching the end of the obscurity, but the light confused me and bathed everything in mysterious, frightening colors.

The silence was now complete, and as I noticed this, I heard, coming from my left, a woman's voice. I stopped immediately, expecting to hear it again, but I heard nothing—not even the normal sounds of the forest, with its crickets, its insects, and its animals walking through the dry leaves. I looked at my watch: it was exactly 5:15 P.M. I estimated that I was still about three miles from Tricastela and that there was still time to arrive before dark.

As I looked up from my watch, I heard the woman's voice again. And from that point on, I was to live through one of the most significant experiences of my life.

The voice wasn't coming from somewhere in the woods but from somewhere inside me. I was able to hear it clearly, and it heightened my intuitive sense. It was neither I nor Astrain who was speaking. The voice only told me that I should keep on walking, which I did unquestioningly. It was as if Petrus had returned and was telling me again about giving orders and taking them. At that moment, I was simply an instrument of the Road; the Road was indeed "walking me." The fog grew less and less dense; I seemed to be walking out of it. Around me were the bare trees, the moist and slippery terrain, and ahead of me, the same steep slope I had been climbing for such a long time.

Suddenly, as if by magic, the fog lifted completely. And there before me, driven into the crest of the mountain, was a cross.

I looked around, and I could see both the fog bank from which I had emerged and another above me. Between the two, I could see the peaks of the tallest mountains and the top of El Cebrero, where the cross was. I felt a strong desire to pray. Even though I knew that I would have to detour from the road to Tricastela, I decided to climb to the peak and say my prayers at the foot of the cross. It took forty minutes to make the climb, and I did it in complete silence, within and without. The language I had invented was forgotten; it was not the right language for communicating with other people or with God. The Road to Santiago was "walking me," and it was going to show me where my sword was. Petrus was right again.

When I reached the peak, a man was sitting there, writing something. For an instant I thought he was a supernatural being, sent from elsewhere. Then my intuition told me that he was not, and I saw the scallop shell stitched into his clothing; he was just a pilgrim, who looked at me for a few moments and then walked away, disturbed by my having appeared. Perhaps he had been expecting the same thing as I — an angel—and we had each found just another person on the Road of the common people.

Although I wanted to pray, I wasn't able to say anything. I stood in front of the cross for some time, looking at the mountains and at the clouds that covered the sky and the land, leaving only the high peaks clear. Thirty yards below me there was a hamlet with fifteen houses and a small church, whose lights were being turned on. At least I had somewhere to spend the night if the Road told me to do so. I was not sure when it would tell me, but even with Petrus gone, I was not without a guide. The Road was "walking me."

An unfettered lamb, climbing the mountain, stopped between the cross and me. He looked at me, a bit frightened. For some time I stood there, looking at the black sky, and the cross, and the white lamb at its foot. All at once, I felt exhausted by all that time spent on tests and battles and lessons and the pilgrimage. I felt a terrible pain in my stomach, and it rose to my throat, where it was transformed into dry, tearless sobs. There I stood, overcome by the scene of the lamb and the cross. This was a cross that I need not set upright, for it was there before me, solitary and immense, resisting time and the elements. It was a symbol of the fate that people created, not for their God but for themselves. The lessons of the Road to Santiago came back to me as I sobbed there, with a frightened lamb as my witness.

"My Lord," I said, finally able to pray, "I am not nailed to this cross, nor do I see you there. The cross is empty, and that is how it should stay forever; the time of death is already past, and a god is now reborn within me. This cross is the symbol of the infinite power that each of us has. Now this power is reborn, the world is saved, and I am able to perform your miracles, because I trod the Road of the common people and, in mingling with them, found your secret. You came among us to teach us all that we were capable of becoming, and we did not want to accept this. You showed us that the power and the glory were within every person's reach, and this sudden vision of our capacity was too much for us. We crucified you, not because we were ungrateful to the Son of God but because we were fearful of accepting our own capacity. We crucified you fearing that we might be transformed into gods. With time and tradition, you came to be just a distant divinity, and we returned to our destiny as human beings.

"It is not a sin to be happy. Half a dozen exercises and an attentive ear are enough to allow us to realize our most impossible dreams. Because of my pride in wisdom, you made me walk the Road that every person can walk, and discover what everyone else already knows if they have paid the slightest attention to life. You made me see that the search for happiness is a personal search and not a model we can pass on to others. Before finding my sword, I had to discover its secret— and the secret was so simple; it was to know what to do with it. With it and with the happiness that it would represent to me.

"I have walked so many miles to discover things I already knew, things that all of us know but that are so hard to accept. Is there anything harder for us, my Lord, than discovering that we can achieve the power? This pain that I feel now in my breast, that makes me sob and that frightens that poor lamb, has been felt since human beings first existed. Few can accept the burden of their own victory: most give up their dreams when they see that they can be realized. They refuse to fight the good fight because they do not know what to do with their own happiness; they are imprisoned by the things of the world. Just as I have been, who wanted to find my sword without knowing what to do with it."

A god sleeping within me was awakening, and the pain was growing worse and worse. I felt the presence close to me of my Master, and I was able for the first time to turn my sobs into tears. I wept with gratitude for his having made me search for my sword along the Road to Santiago. I wept with gratitude for Petrus, for his having taught me, without saying a word, that I would realize my dreams if I first discovered what I wanted to do with them. I saw the cross, with no one on it, and the lamb at its base, free to go where he wanted in those mountains and to see the clouds above his head and below his feet.

The lamb began to walk away, and I followed him. I already knew where he would lead me; in spite of the clouds, everything had become clear to me. Even if I could not see the Milky Way in the sky, I was certain that it was there, pointing the way along the Road to Santiago. I followed the lamb as he walked in the direction of the hamlet—which was called El Cebrero, like the mountain.

There, at one time, a miracle had happened. It was the miracle of transforming what you do into what you believe in, just like the secret of my sword and of the Strange Road to Santiago. As we descended the mountain, I remembered the story. A farmer from a nearby village had climbed the mountain to attend mass at El Cebrero on a stormy day. The mass was being celebrated by a monk who was almost completely lacking in faith and who ridiculed the farmer for having made such an effort to get there. But at the moment of consecration, the host had actually been transformed into the body of Christ and the wine into his blood. The relics are still there, guarded in that small chapel, a treasure greater than all the riches of the Vatican.

The lamb stopped at the edge of the hamlet, where there was only one street leading to the church. At that moment, I was seized by a terrible fear, and I began to repeat over and over, "Lord, I am not worthy to enter thy house." But the lamb looked at me and spoke to me through his eyes. He said that I should forget forever my unworthiness because the power had been reborn in me, in the same way that it could be reborn in all people who devoted their lives to the good fight. A day would come—said the lamb's eyes—when people would once again take pride in themselves, and then all of nature would praise the awakening of the God that had been sleeping within them.

As the lamb looked at me, I could read all of this in his eyes; now he had become my guide along the Road to Santiago. For a moment everything went dark, and I began to see scenes that were reminiscent of those I had read about in the Apocalypse: the Great Lamb on his throne and people washing his vestments, cleansing them with his blood. This was the moment when the God was awakened in each of them. I also saw the wars and hard times and catastrophes that were going to shake the earth over the next few years. But everything ended with the victory of the Lamb and with every human being on earth awakening the sleeping God and all of God's power.

I followed the lamb to the small chapel built by the farmer and by the monk who had come to believe in what he did. Nobody knows who they were. Two nameless tombstones in the cemetery by the chapel mark the place where they were buried. But it is impossible to tell which is the grave of the monk and which of the farmer. The miracle had occurred because both had fought the good fight.

The chapel was completely lit when I came to its door. Yes, I was worthy of entering, because I had a sword and I knew what to do with it. These were not the Gates of

Forgiveness, because I had already been forgiven and had washed my clothing in the blood of the Lamb. Now I wanted only to hold my sword and go out to fight the good fight.

In the small church there was no cross. There on the altar were the relics of the miracle: the chalice and the paten that I had seen during the dance, and a silver reliquary containing the body and blood of Jesus. I once again believed in miracles and in the impossible things that human beings can accomplish in their daily lives. The mountain peaks seemed to say to me that they were there only as a challenge to humans—and that humans exist only to accept the honor of that challenge.

The lamb slipped into one of the pews, and I looked to the front of the chapel. Standing before the altar, smiling—and perhaps a bit relieved—was my Master: with my sword in his hand.

I stopped, and he came toward me, passing me by and going outside. I followed him. In front of the chapel, looking up at the dark sky, he unsheathed my sword and told me to grasp its hilt with him. He pointed the blade upward and said the sacred Psalm of those who travel far to achieve victory:

A thousand fall at your side, and ten thousand to your right, but you will not be touched.
No evil will befall you, no curse will fall upon your tent;
your angels will be given orders regarding you,
to protect you along your every way.

I knelt, and as he touched the blade to my shoulders, he said:

Trample the lion and the serpent,
The lion cub and the dragon will make shoes for your feet.

As he finished saying this, it began to rain. The rain fertilized the earth, and its water would return to the sky after having given birth to a seed, grown a tree, brought a flower into blossom. The storm intensified, and I raised my head, feeling the rain for the first time in my entire journey along the Road to Santiago. I remembered the dry fields, and I was joyful that they were being showered upon that night. I remembered the rocks in León, the wheat fields of Navarra, the dryness of Castile, and the vineyards of Rioja that today were drinking the rain that fell in torrents, with all of the force in the skies. I remembered having raised a cross, and I thought that the storm would once again cause it to fall to earth so that another pilgrim could learn about command and obedience. I thought of the waterfall, which now must be even stronger because of the rainfall, and of Foncebadon, where I had left such power to fertilize the soil again. I thought about all of the water I had drunk from so many fountains that were now being replenished. I was worthy of my sword because I knew what to do with it.

The Master held out the sword to me, and I grasped it. I looked about for the lamb, but he had disappeared. But that did not matter: the Water of Life fell from the sky and caused the blade of my sword to glisten.

Epilogue

Santiago de Compostela

From the window of my hotel I can see the Cathedral of Santiago and the tourists at its main gate. Students in black medieval clothing mingle with the townspeople, and the souvenir vendors are setting up their stalls. It is early in the morning, and except for my notes, these are the first lines I have written about the Road to Santiago.

I reached the city yesterday, after having caught the bus that runs from Pedrafita, near El Cebrero, to Compostela. In four hours we covered the 150 kilometers that separate the two cities, and this reminded me of the journey with Petrus. At times, it took us two weeks to cover that distance. In a short while, I am going to the tomb of San Tiago to leave there the image of Our Lady of the Visitation, mounted on the scallop shells. Then, as soon as possible, I am going to catch a plane for Brazil, because I have a lot to do. I remember that Petrus told me once that he had condensed all of his experience into one picture, and the thought occurs to me that I might write a book about everything that has happened to me. But this is still a remote idea; I have so much to do now that I have recovered my sword.

The secret of my sword is mine, and I will never reveal it to anyone. I wrote it down and left it under a stone, but with the rain, the paper has probably been destroyed. It's better that way. Petrus didn't need to know.

I asked my Master whether he had known what day I was going to arrive or whether he had been waiting there for some time. He laughed and said that he had arrived there the morning before and was going to leave the next day, whether I appeared or not.

I asked how that was possible, and he did not answer me. But when we were saying good-bye and he was getting into the rental car that would take him back to Madrid, he gave me a small medal of the Order of San Tiago of the Sword. And he told me that I had already had a great revelation when I had looked into the eyes of the lamb.

And when I think about it, I guess it is true that people always arrive at the right moment at the place where someone awaits them.

THE ALCHEMIST
Paulo Coelho

Every few decades a book is published that changes the lives of its readers forever. Paulo Coelho's *The Alchemist* is such a book. With over 27 million copies sold worldwide, *The Alchemist* has already achieved the status of a modern classic.

This is the story of Santiago, an Andalusian shepherd boy who dreams of travelling the world in search of a treasure as extravagant as any ever found. From his home in Spain he journeys to the exotic markets of Tangiers and then into the Egyptian desert, where a fateful encounter with the alchemist awaits him.

The Alchemist is a transforming novel about the essential wisdom of listening to our hearts, learning to read the omens strewn along life's path and, above all, following our dreams.

BY THE RIVER PIEDRA
I SAT DOWN AND WEPT
Paulo Coelho

By the River Piedra tells the story of Pilar, an independent and practical yet restless young woman, who is frustrated by the daily grind of university life and looking for greater meaning in her life. Pilar is transformed forever by an encounter with a childhood friend, now a mesmerizing and handsome spiritual teacher — and a rumoured miracle worker — who leads her on a journey through the French Pyrenees, a magical landscape that has been home to holy visions and miracles through the ages.

THE FIFTH MOUNTAIN
Paulo Coelho

Fleeing his home from persecution, 23-year-old Elijah takes refuge with a young widow and her son in the beautiful town of Akbar. Already struggling to maintain his sanity in a chaotic world of tyranny and war, he is now forced to choose between his new-found love and his overwhelming sense of duty.

Evoking all the drama and intrigue of the colourful, chaotic world of the Middle East, Paulo Coelho turns the trials of Elijah into an intensely moving and inspiring story – one that powerfully brings out the universal themes of how faith and love can ultimately triumph over suffering.

THE PILGRIMAGE
Paulo Coelho

On a legendary road across Spain, travelled by pilgrims of San Tiago, we find Paulo Coelho on a contemporary quest for ancient wisdom. This journey becomes a truly initiatory experience, and Paulo is transformed forever as he learns to understand the nature of truth through the simplicity of life.

The Pilgrimage has a very important place in the work of Paulo Coelho, not just because it is the first of his major books, but because of the way in which it expresses the humanity of Paulo's philosophy and the depth of his search.

VERONIKA DECIDES TO DIE
Paulo Coelho

Veronika seems to have everything she could wish for. She is young and pretty, has plenty of attractive boyfriends, goes dancing, has a steady job, a loving family. Yet Veronika is not happy; something is lacking in her life. On the morning of November 11th, 1997, she decides to die. She takes an overdose of sleeping pills, only to wake up some time later in Villete, the local hospital. There she is told that although she is alive now her heart is damaged and she has only a few days to live …

This story follows Veronika through these intense days as, to her surprise, she finds herself drawn into the enclosed world of Villete. She begins to notice more, to become interested in the other patients. She starts to see her past relationships much more clearly and understand why she had felt her life had no meaning. In this heightened state, Veronika discovers things she has never really allowed herself to feel before: hatred, fear, curiosity, love — even sexual awakening. Against all odds, she finds she is falling in love and wanting, if at all possible, to live again …

THE DEVIL AND MISS PRYM
Paulo Coelho

A stranger arrives in the small mountain village of Viscos. He carries with him a backpack containing a notebook and eleven gold bars. He comes searching for the answer to a question that torments him: are human beings, in essence, good or evil? In welcoming the mysterious foreigner, the whole village becomes an accomplice to his sophisticated plot, which will forever mark their lives.

In this stunning new novel, Paulo Coelho's unusual protagonist sets the town a moral challenge from which they may never recover. A fascinating meditation on the human soul, *The Devil and Miss Prym* illuminates the reality of good and evil within us all, and our uniquely human capacity to choose between them.

MANUAL OF THE WARRIOR OF LIGHT
Paulo Coelho

Manual of the Warrior of Light is an invitation to each of us to live our dream, to embrace the uncertainty of life and to rise to meet our own unique destiny. In his inimitable style, Paulo Coelho helps us to discover the warrior of light within each of us.

With inspiring short passages, we are invited to embark upon the way of the warrior: the one who appreciates the miracle of being alive, the one who accepts failure and the one whose quest leads him to become the person he wants to be.

ELEVEN MINUTES
Paulo Coelho

Eleven Minutes tells the story of Maria, a young girl from a Brazilian village, whose first innocent brushes with love leave her heart-broken. At a tender age, she becomes convinced that she will never find true love, instead believing that 'Love is a terrible thing that will make you suffer ...' A chance meeting in Rio takes her to Geneva, where she dreams of finding fame and fortune yet ends up working as a prostitute.

In Geneva, Maria drifts further and further away from love while at the same time developing a fascination with sex. Eventually Maria's despairing view of love is put to the test when she meets a handsome young painter. In the odyssey of self-discovery, Maria has to choose between pursuing a path of darkness, sexual pleasure for its own sake, or risking everything to find her own 'inner light' and the possibility of sacred sex, sex in the context of love.

In this gripping and daring new novel, Paulo Coelho sensitively explores the sacred nature of sex and love and invites us to confront our own prejudices and demons and embrace our own 'inner light'.

www.harpercollins.co.uk/coelho

For the latest information on

Paulo Coelho, excerpts from his

books and exclusive competitions,

visit our website.